BRADBURY

FAHRENHEIT 451

NOTES

COLES EDITORIAL BOARD

Bound to stay open

Publisher's Note

Otabind (Ota-bind). This book has been bound using the patented Otabind process. You can open this book at any page, gently run your finger down the spine, and the pages will lie flat.

ABOUT COLES NOTES

COLES NOTES have been an indispensible aid to students on five continents since 1948.

COLES NOTES are available for a wide range of individual literary works. Clear, concise explanations and insights are provided along with interesting interpretations and evaluations.

Proper use of COLES NOTES will allow the student to pay greater attention to lectures and spend less time taking notes. This will result in a broader understanding of the work being studied and will free the student for increased participation in discussions.

COLES NOTES are an invaluable aid for review and exam preparation as well as an invitation to explore different interpretive paths.

COLES NOTES are written by experts in their fields. It should be noted that any literary judgement expressed herein is just that — the judgement of one school of thought. Interpretations that diverge from, or totally disagree with any criticism may be equally valid.

COLES NOTES are designed to supplement the text and are not intended as a substitute for reading the text itself. Use of the NOTES will serve not only to clarify the work being studied, but should enhance the reader's enjoyment of the topic.

ISBN 0-7740-3288-X

© COPYRIGHT 1992 AND PUBLISHED BY
COLES PUBLISHING COMPANY
TORONTO—CANADA
PRINTED IN CANADA

Manufactured by Webcom Limited
Cover finish: Webcom's Exclusive **Duracoat**

CONTENTS

THE AUTHOR

Ray Douglas Bradbury was born on August 22, 1920, in the town of Waukegan, Illinois. His grandfather and great-grandfather came from a long line of editors and publishers, and there was a family publishing firm, known as Bradbury and Sons. On his father's side, the family was descended from forebears who came to the United States in 1630. His mother was born in Stockholm, Sweden; the family moved to the United States in 1890. Bradbury remained in Waukegan, and attended public school there, until 1934, when the family moved to California.

Bradbury has described his aunt, Neva Bradbury, as being a major influence in his childhood years, for she used to read to him. However, in this period there was another influence whose impact is obvious. At the age of eight, Ray Bradbury discovered Buck Rogers in the comic pages of the newspaper. A new world, peopled with Buck Rogers, Flash Gordon, Tarzan and the characters from *Amazing Stories*, suddenly began to open up to him. In his own words he became "aware of the fabulous world of the future, and the world of fantasy." The impact of that world upon the young boy has been described by Bradbury himself:

> I lived completely in a world of fantasy and illusion, collecting Buck Rogers and Flash Gordon comic strips, doing magic shows, appearing in plays, reading the comics to children over a radio station in Arizona, and writing my first stories on my toy machine, profusely illustrated.

Some idea of his precociousness in the world of illusion can be gained from the realization that he had become a boy magician by the age of twelve and had received his first typewriter—a toy—for his twelfth birthday!

The high-school period in Los Angeles was no less productive. At the age of fifteen, he began submitting—unsuccessfully—stories to various magazines, such as *The Saturday Evening Post*, *Collier's* and *Esquire*. In the last year before high-school graduation, he joined the Los Angeles Science-Fiction Society and started writing science-fiction stories for his own magazine, *Futuria Fantasia*, which, however, lasted for only four issues.

In view of Bradbury's passion for writing, and dealing with illusion and the future, it is not surprising that he sought to devote himself to writing upon leaving high school. For three years after graduating from high school, he sold newspapers on street corners in order to finance himself while he wrote. And he wrote steadily; during this period he wrote between one- and two-thousand words a day, most of which he later burned! However, his persistence brought its rewards. His first published story, "It's not the Heat, it's the Hu", appeared in *Script* magazine in 1940. He was not paid for the work, but at least he had finally appeared in print. His successes followed, seemingly almost inevitably. The first story for which he was paid was published in *Super Science Stories* in 1941. Concentrating on the popular, "pulp" magazines of the day, he compiled an impressive list of credits. Even a list of magazine titles is impressive. Between 1941 and 1945, his stories were published in the following magazines: *Weird Tales*, *Amazing Stories*, *Astounding Science Fiction*, *Thrilling Wonder Stories*, *Astonishing*, and *Captain Future*. This laid the foundation for his appearance in higher-quality magazines, and his stories were soon published in *American Mercury*, *Charm*, *Mademoiselle*, and *Colliers*. The titles of the magazines give an accurate indication of the wide audience to whom Bradbury's stories appealed.

Bradbury had good reason to be satisfied with the results of his labours. However, his writing is not simply an expression of his egotism, or simply an expression of his desire for financial rewards. His interest in, and concentration upon, fantasy in writing springs from a genuine appreciation of what can be accomplished by that *genre*. As he himself has expressed it, "I think that science fiction and fantasy offer the liveliest, freshest approaches to many of our problems today, and I always hope to write in this vivid and vigorous form, saying that I think about philosophy and sociology in our immediate future." In his concept of his craft, Bradbury conceives the world of fantasy as offering the writer the opportunity to exercise what he feels to be his social responsibility. Fantasy, according to this concept, does not mean fairy-tale; it is a mode with powerful social relevance.

Ray Bradbury is still a resident of California, living in Los Angeles. He is the father of two daughters, having married Marguerite Susan (McClure) Bradbury, on September 27, 1947. Mrs. Bradbury was an English instructor at the University College of Los Angeles.

It would be a formidable task to list all of Mr. Bradbury's published works, for his production has been prolific. Some of his more important works are as follows:

1947   *Dark Carnival*
1950   *The Martian Chronicles*
1951   *The Illustrated Man*

1953	*The Golden Apples of the Sun*
1953	*Fahrenheit 451*
1955	*Switch on the Night*

The list could be extended exhaustively, for there are as many favourite Bradbury stories as there are Bradbury readers. *The October Country*, *Tomorrow Midnight* and *The Autumn People*—all stories involving fantasy—are later favourites. All reveal Bradbury's passionate concept of the *genre* he has chosen;

> . . . Science-fiction is a wonderful hammer; I intend to use it when and if necessary, to bark a few shins or knock a few heads, in order to make people leave people alone.

(*NOTE*: The source for much of the biographical material in this section is: KUNITZ, S. J. (ed.) *Twentieth-Century Authors*, First Supplement. New York: The H. W. Wilson Co., 1955)

DETAILED SUMMARIES

PART ONE: THE HEARTH AND THE SALAMANDER

p. 3 *"It was a pleasure to burn."*

Montag, the fireman, reflected that it was "a special pleasure" to see things consumed by fire. With his helmet, bearing its symbolic number 451, on his head and his eyes "all orange flame", he felt like the conductor of an orchestra as his fire-hose reduced to ruins a house and its books. As he worked, he "grinned the fierce grin of all men singed and driven back by flame."

He knew that when he returned to the firehouse he might wink at his burnt-cork image in the mirror, and that later, drifting off to sleep, his face would wear the ever-present smile.

p. 4 *"He hung up his black beetle-colored helmet . . ."*

He stored away his uniform carefully, showered and, whistling, left the station. The subway train wafted him silently to the suburb where he lived.

Still whistling, he emerged into the night air and walked towards the corner. Before he reached the corner, he slowed down. The last few nights he had felt, just before turning the corner, that someone had been there. It was a feeling he could not explain, because each night the sidewalk had in fact been empty. Tonight, however, he slowed almost to a stop.

He turned the corner and encountered a girl dressed in white and having a "slender and milk-white" face. She was Clarisse McClellan, Guy Montag's new neighbour. As he talked to her, Montag felt that there seemed to be "the faintest breath of fresh apricots and strawberries in the air", though he knew that that was impossible so late in the year. Moreover, as he talked to her he felt disturbed, as though she were "turning him end for end, shaking him quietly, and emptying his pockets, without once moving herself."

Clarisse was seventeen and crazy: two things, which according to her uncle, always go together. Her dark eyes and her fragile face, "with a soft and constant light in it", held Montag. He was reminded of a moment in his childhood during a power failure, when his mother had lighted a last candle and mother and son together had savoured "the strangely comfortable and rare and gently flattering light."

Clarisse declared that she was not afraid of Montag, though he was a fireman, and she asked him questions about his work. He revealed that he had been a fireman for ten years, since he was twenty. He never read any of the books he burned, for that was against the law. To him, it was "fine work." He laughed at her suggestion that long ago firemen used to put fires out instead of starting them because, he declared, houses had always been fireproof.

The girl and Montag were very different. She regretted the speed of the jet-cars which made the drivers unable to see the beauty through which they drove. She rarely watched the 'parlor walls' or went to races or to Fun Parks. She reminded Montag of the dew on the grass in the morning, and of the man in the moon. He, in contrast, had not looked around himself for a long time. As a result, they walked the rest of the way in silence, his being "a kind of clenching and uncomfortable silence in which he shot her accusing glances."

When they reached her house, all its lights were blazing, a fact which astonished Montag. Clarisse declared that no doubt her mother and father and her uncle were sitting around talking. She laughed when Montag asked what they found to talk about. As she turned to leave him, she asked a final question: "Are you happy?"

p. 9 *"Happy! Of all the nonsense."*

As Montag entered his house, he insisted to himself that of course he was happy. As he pondered their meeting, he moved his eyes quickly away from the ventilator grille in the hall, having remembered that something lay hidden behind it. It had been a strange meeting, something like that with an old man in the park a year ago, when they had talked.

Though impatient with his other self, "the subconscious idiot that ran babbling at times, quite independent of will, habit, and conscience," Montag could not forget the girl's face. Unlike the faces of others, it had seemed to reflect his own "innermost trembling thought." She had possessed an "incredible power of identification", so that she anticipated his gestures before he even made them. Their meeting had lasted only a few minutes, yet that time seemed large now. And, he reflected, she had almost seemed to be waiting for him.

p. 10 *"He opened the bedroom door."*

Montag entered the bedroom, which seemed like "the cold marbled room of a mausoleum." There was complete darkness. The only sound was the tiny hum of the thimble radios which, he knew, his wife would have in her ears, for Mildred had been lulled to sleep by their music every night for two years now.

As he approached the bed, his foot struck a small object and sent it sliding away. He lighted his igniter to look at his wife. Her breathing was faint, and her eyes were like glass. He now saw the object he had kicked; it was an empty bottle of sleeping capsules which earlier that day had contained thirty tablets. Montag shrieked and plunged toward the telephone. He called the emergency hospital, feeling that the roar of jet aircraft overhead had pulverized the stars.

His agony was a reminder of that moment when he had entered the bedroom. For then he had confessed that he was not happy. The girl next door had robbed him of his mask of happiness.

p. 13 *"They had this machine."*

The operators from the hospital had two machines with which they worked on Mildred. One machine descended into the stomach, searching the area with its Eye and pumping out the poison; the other replaced all the blood in the body with fresh blood and serum.

The impersonal operators, "men with the eyes of puff adders", were unmoved by Montag's anger. He was distressed that neither of the operators was a doctor. However, as they explained, there were nine or ten cases like that of Mildred every night, and a doctor was not needed to operate the machines.

Alone, Montag waited for Mildred to recover. The problem, he thought, was that everyone was a stranger. "Nobody knows anyone." Mildred, he observed, looked refreshed with the new blood. He wished that her mind could have been refreshed as well as her blood. For now, at two o'clock in the morning and only one hour after meeting Clarisse, it seemed as though "the world had melted down and sprung up in a new and colorless form."

Drawn by the sound of relaxed laughter from the McClelland house, Montag stepped out of the French windows and stood outside the "talking house." He wanted to ask to be let in, but remained outside, listening to a voice which observed that this was the age of disposable people.

Montag returned to his house and lay down to sleep, his mind in a turmoil. As he dissolved a sleeping tablet on his tongue, he reflected that he did not know anything anymore.

p. 16 *"At nine in the morning . . ."*

Next morning, Mildred's bed was empty when Montag awoke. His heart pumping, he entered the kitchen. His wife was having break-fast, the Seashell thimbles in her ears. Being an expert lip-reader because of her addiction to the thimbles, she conversed with Montag, revealing that she remembered nothing of the night before. Her only symptoms were hunger, a hangover and a sore stomach.

p. 17 *"In the late afternoon . . ."*

In the late afternoon, preparing to go to work, Montag confronted Mildred with what she had done the night before. She refused to believe that she had taken the bottle of sleeping tablets.

Mildred was more engrossed in her television script, which enabled her to take part in that afternoon's programme on the wall-to-wall circuit. The play was written with one part missing, and the homemaker was asked to read the missing lines. Although Montag was still paying for the third television wall which had been installed only two months previously, Mildred wanted the fourth wall, for then "it'd be just like this room wasn't ours at all, but all kinds of exotic people's rooms."

Montag left his house and walked out into the rain.

p. 19 *"The rain was thinning away . . ."*

Outside, Clarisse was walking in the rain. In her hand, she held the last of the year's dandelions. Holding it under her chin, she told Montag that if the yellow rubbed off it meant that she was in love. Intrigued, he found that the yellow showed under her chin. When Clarisse held the flower under his chin, no yellow showed and she declared that he was not in love with anyone. Upset, Montag insisted that he was in love.

Clarisse revealed that she was made to visit a psychiatrist, who wanted to know what she did with her time and why she walked in the forests watching birds and collecting butterflies. Montag confessed that he found her peculiar and aggravating, for though his wife was thirty, Clarisse at times seemed much older than Mildred.

Clarisse began to ask Montag questions about his work, because she found him different from other firemen. When he talked to her, he looked at her; and when she had mentioned the moon, he had looked at the moon. The others would not have done that. They would have left her or threatened her. That is why she found it strange that Montag should be a fireman. As she talked, Montag felt his body divide into two halves, one a "softness", the other a "hard-ness."

When she left him, he stood still for a long time. When he moved at last, he walked slowly and opened his mouth to taste the rain, just as she had done.

p. 22 *"The Mechanical Hound slept . . ."*

Downstairs in the firehouse, in a dark corner, the Mechanical Hound lay in its illuminated kennel. Here and there the light of one in the morning touched on the metal of the machine, whose olfactory system could be set to catch and destroy various animals. On quiet nights, the firemen would let loose rats or chickens or cats and bet on which animal would be caught first by the machine. Two years ago, Montag had been one of the keenest gamblers, having once lost a week's salary in the sport. Now he stayed upstairs most nights, listening to the sounds of the game.

Montag, "fascinated as always with the dead beast, the living beast," touched its muzzle. He jumped back as it growled. The Hound half rose and looked at him. Its four-inch steel needle, which injected its prey with massive doses of morphine or procaine, pulsated. As the Hound stepped from its kennel, Montag grabbed the brass pole which whisked him upstairs. On the upstairs deck, he trembled, his face green-white.

On the upper level, four men were playing cards. Only one of them, the Captain, looked at Montag with curiosity. Montag declared that the Hound did not like him, but the Captain stated that the beast could not like or dislike, for, like a machine, it was simply set to carry out its functions. Montag reminded him that the beast's calculators could be set to any combination of chemical balances, and that the combinations of all the firemen were recorded in the master files downstairs; it would, then, be easy, he declared, for anyone to set the machine to the correct combinations. That, he claimed, might account for the Hound's reaction to him. Moreover, he continued, the Hound had reacted the same way twice last month. As the Captain promised to have the machine checked, Montag thought uneasily about the ventilator grille at home and what lay hidden behind it. If someone at the firehouse knew about it, he might have "told" the Hound.

Still curious, Captain Beatty approached Montag, who wondered what the beast thought about at nights and whether or not it was coming alive. Beatty objected that the beast only thought what they wanted it to think. This, Montag countered, was a pity, since then it could only know hunting and finding and killing. Since it found its target unerringly, he would not want to be its next victim. The

Captain asked him if he had a guilty conscience, and began to laugh softly.

p. 25 *"One two three . . ."*

Days passed. As often as Montag came out of the house, he saw Clarisse. On a number of occasions she left flowers or other small tokens on his porch. Every day she walked him to the corner.

Once he asked her why it was that he felt he had known her for years, and she explained that there were three reasons: she liked him; she did not want anything from him; and they knew one another. When Clarisse asked him why he did not have children of his own, since he loved children so much, Montag had to explain that Mildred did not want children. However, he did not mind the question, for it had been a long time since anyone cared enough to ask.

Clarisse went on to declare that his laugh sounded much nicer than it had. Feeling at ease and comfortable, Montag asked her why she was not in school that day. She replied that she was not missed because she was thought to be antisocial. To Clarisse, being social was talking to Montag or to other people. She did not think it social to be always involved in organized group activities, so that in the end people were 'run so ragged' that they could not do anything except "go to bed or head for a Fun Park to bully people around, break windowpanes in the Window Smasher place or wreck cars in the Car Wrecker place with the big steel ball." The world, she declared, was too violent, with people her own age killing one another. Her uncle had told her that her grandfather said that at one time children did not kill one another. At any rate, she was different, for she was brought up to be responsible, and was spanked when she needed it and did the shopping and housecleaning by hand. Most of all, however, she liked to watch people and wonder about them. But she had discovered that people did not really say anything to one another; they simply engaged in mechanical activities, with even art being depersonalized.

p. 29 *"One two three . . ."*

At the firehouse, Montag's behaviour was a little unusual: he climbed up the firemen's pole; and he entered by the back door, seemingly because he was afraid of the Hound. He was told that in Seattle a fireman had committed suicide strangely, by setting a Mechanical Hound to his own chemical complex and letting it loose.

Suddenly, Clarisse was gone. The breaking of the routine of meeting with her disturbed him.

p. 29 *"The flutter of cards . . ."*

At the firehouse, Montag played cards with the other firemen, but his mind was working "behind the barrier he had momentarily erected" by closing his eyes. Suddenly a voice broke in upon him, cutting across the sound of a radio talking about the imminence of war. Startled, Montag looked at his companions and wondered whether all firemen had "black hair, black brows, a fiery face, and a blue-steel shaved but unshaved look." Montag explained that he had been wondering what happened to the man whose library they had burned last week. He was told that the man had been taken to an asylum. When Montag countered that the man had not seemed to be insane, he was met with the response that anyone who thought he could fool the government and the firemen must be insane.

Montag persisted by wondering aloud how they would feel if firemen burned their houses and books. Captain Beatty quickly asked whether Montag had any books, and he hurriedly denied that he had, though the thought of the ventilator grille at home came into his mind. Montag, remembering Clarisse, further wondered aloud whether firemen had once put out fires. However, Stoneman and Black dismissed his question, by quoting from their rule books, which stated that the firemen had been established in 1790 to burn English-influenced books, and that the First Fireman had been Benjamin Franklin.

An alarm interrupted the conversation. However, Montag went down the pole like a man in a dream. As the Mechanical Hound leaped up in its kennel, Montag was reminded that he had forgotten his helmet. With siren screaming, the engine left on its call.

p. 32 *"It was a flaking three-story house . . ."*

The call was to a century-old house in the old part of the city. Its thin fireproof plastic coating seemed to be the only thing holding it together. Inside, an old woman stood weaving from side to side, as though in a trance. Beatty slapped her and asked where the books were. Having been advised by the woman's neighbour to check the attic, the firemen swung their axes in the "musty blackness." A "fountain of books" fell upon Montag as he climbed the stairs. He shuddered, for the woman's presence was discomforting. Previously, the police had gagged the victim and removed him before the firemen arrived, so that the firemen's work had seemed simply like "cleaning up." Now, Montag felt that his companions were too noisy and the woman too accusingly silent.

As the books cascaded forth, one of them fluttered into Montag's arms and one line from it burned itself upon his mind: "Time has fallen asleep in the afternoon sunshine." As though acting independently, Montag's hand swept the book under his armpit.

As the men splashed the books with kerosene, they tried to persuade the old woman to leave the house. She refused. Finally, the firemen fled when she opened her hand and showed them a kitchen match. As they watched from the lawn, she struck the match contemptuously on the railing of the porch. Beatty did not need to ignite the trail of kerosene.

p. 36 *"They said nothing . . ."*

On the return journey, the firemen stared quietly out of the front of the great Salamander. Montag tried to recall what the woman had said as they entered the house. Captain Beatty was able to recall the words—"Play the man, Master Ridley; we shall this day light such a candle, by God's grace in England, as I trust shall never be put out."—and informed Montag that a man named Latimer had spoken the words to a man named Nicholas Ridley as they were being burnt alive at Oxford, for heresy, on October 16, 1555.

Stoneman missed the corner where they should have turned for the firehouse.

p. 37 *"Who is it?"*

At home once more, Mildred called to Montag to put out the light and come to bed. As he thought of the book he had brought from the old woman's house, Montag felt strange, as though his hand had infected his entire body with a poison. In the darkness, he stuffed the book under his pillow.

For a short while, Mildred and he engaged in inconsequential talk. At last he fell silent. He felt his wife move and approach his bed. She put her hand on his cheek. He knew that when she drew it away it was wet.

p. 38 *"Late in the night . . ."*

Late at night, Montag looked over at his wife. She was awake, staring into the darkness, the Seashell in her ear. In order to communicate with her, he thought of buying a Seashell broadcasting station. But what could he say to her?

She suddenly seemed strange to him. He felt as though he were in someone else's house. He asked her if she could remember when and where they had met. Though he reminded her that it had happened ten years ago, she could recall nothing of their meeting. She dismissed his question with a laugh, but to Montag it meant a great deal suddenly that they should remember.

Mildred rose and went to the bathroom to take more pills. As she swallowed them, Montag recalled the grim visit of the men who had rescued her when she had taken an overdose. He remembered thinking then that if she died, he would not cry. For he was simply "a silly empty man near a silly empty woman." He wondered how one became so empty. Clarisse's dandelion had summed it up: he was not in love with anyone. Why not?

There was a wall between himself and Mildred. In fact, there were three walls between them—the television walls. They were three expensive walls peopled by "the gibbering pack of tree-apes that said nothing, nothing, nothing and said it loud, loud, loud." Thus his most significant memory of Mildred was of her sitting in the midst of the living room, which was aptly named, for the walls were always talking to her. On the screen, the "family" would be quarrelling. Mildred did not know what the quarrel was about, or with whom they were angry, or what they were going to do. He had waited to see, but had been overcome by "a great thunderstorm of sound" from the walls. The effect was that of drowning in music and noise. Something had happened, but he did not know what. Mildred still could not explain it. To Montag, nothing was connected. To Mildred, it was sufficient to know that the people on the screen fought a lot, and they were married.

If he did not think of the three walls soon to be four, he thought of Mildred driving across town at a hundred miles an hour. He screeched at her to slow down, but her only response was to go faster. When they stopped, he discovered that the Seashells were stuffed in her ears.

Trying to pierce the "crystal barrier" of the Seashells, he asked Mildred about Clarisse, mentioning that he had not seen her for a few days. After some initial difficulty in recalling the girl, Mildred said that the family had moved and that she thought Clarisse had been run over by a car. She had not told him sooner, because she had forgotten.

Mildred inserted the electric thimble in her ear again and lay down, singing softly under her breath. Outside, Montag felt, there was something "like a breath exhaled upon the window." It was the Hound, he thought.

p. 44 *"He had chills and fever in the morning."*

In the morning, Montag was unwell. Mildred stood over his bed, curious. Without opening his eyes, he could imagine her, her hair like straw from chemicals, her eyes with a kind of hidden blindness, her body thin from dieting and her flesh "like white bacon." Montag asked her to bring him aspirin and to turn down the parlor walls. Her favourite program was on, and she made only a pretence of turning it down. She brought him water, but forgot the aspirin.

When she commented that he had acted strangely last night, he told her that the firemen had burned an old lady with her books. Mildred was not really listening, and mentioned that she had watched some of the best programs ever last night. Montag persisted, emphasizing that they had burned a thousand books and a woman last night. But Mildred was more interested in who was going to call Captain Beatty to inform him of Montag's illness. Montag was afraid to do so, because he knew that he would agree to go into work that night. Mildred concluded that Montag was not ill.

Montag suggested that he might quit his job for a while. Mildred objected strongly at his thinking of such a thing because of an old woman who, in any case, was "simple-minded." Montag replied that the memory of that fire would stay with him always, but his wife countered that he should have thought of that when he became a fireman. Since his father and his grandfather had been firemen also, Montag insisted that he had not really had any choice. In any case, he continued, it was not just the old woman. He thought of all the fires over the past ten years and of the fact that behind each book he had burned there stood a man— a man who had taken a long time to put his thoughts down on paper, thoughts which Montag had destroyed in two minutes. Mildred was becoming disturbed by the argument. Though Montag thought it good that they should at last be bothered by something real, he became silent at last, remembering again the visit of the two operators who had saved his wife.

Captain Beatty arrived, for Montag was already two hours late for work, since he was on the early shift that day. The Captain settled himself comfortably, and declared that he knew that Montag was sick and would call in for a day off, for he had "seen it all." He instructed Montag to take the night off.

Beatty explained that every fireman came at some time to feel as Montag felt. Consequently, he declared, it was time for Montag to know the history of his profession. Things had really started, he said, with motion pictures, radio and television in the twentieth-century, five hundred years ago. For the world had become populated with more and more people, and the mass media served to provide them with a mass culture, "a sort of paste pudding norm." With the faster pace of life, books were cut shorter. Condensations and digests were the order of the day, until books became only an entry in a dictionary resumé, and people often had only a vague recollection of the title of a great book. The consequences of the speed-up were enormous: "School is shortened, discipline relaxed, philosophies, histories, languages dropped, English and spelling gradually, gradually neglected." Life became concentrated in the present moment, and man did not need to know anything except how to work his machines. Theatres were emptied, to be replaced by rooms with glass walls and pretty moving colours. More organized sports were provided for the masses; more pictures were provided for their minds. Impatience became the dominant characteristic, with people moving "in nomadic surges from place to place."

As Beatty talked, Mildred left the room, slamming the door, for in adjusting Montag's pillow she found the book he had placed there the night before.

As the population grew, Beatty continued, so did the minorities. The bigger the population, the more minorities. Thus, with the bigger population, the mass media handled controversy less. Consequently, magazines became "a nice blend of vanilla tapioca"; books became "dishwater." The public allowed to survive only the comic books and the sex magazines. No government edict was needed: "Technology, mass exploitation and minority pressure carried the trick." Thus one could stay happy all of the time.

The firemen became important, he continued, as people became more alike. With the schools turning out more activists, intellectuals became feared and hated. Only with "each man the image of every other" could all be happy. In this situation, a book was a threat. Thus, when houses were all fire-proofed, firemen lost their old function and were given a new task, "as custodians of our peace of mind."

Above all, Beatty declared, people want to be happy, and so minorities could not be upset. Fire was the answer to unhappiness. The book that made black people unhappy could be burned; the book that made white people unhappy could be burned. The corpse that made people unhappy could be burned; memorials were simply unhappy reminders.

As Beatty spoke, Mildred appeared in the doorway. She was saying something but could not be heard because of the noise from the parlour walls. Montag lip-read what she was saying, but tried not to look at her in case Beatty turned towards her. Fortunately, she stopped talking just as the "fireworks" in the parlour died down. After a brief pause, Montag asked about Clarisse. Beatty knew of her. The family had been watched for years. The family were regarded as "odd ducks"; and the uncle was branded as antisocial. Beatty regarded the girl as the unfortunate product of the home environment and thought she was better off dead. She had been "embarrassing", for she did not want to know *how* a thing was done, but *why*. Thus, according to Beatty, she was better off dead.

Luckily, Beatty proceeded, the "queer ones" did not happen very often. People were kept happy by keeping them busy at superficial things—contests, parties, entertainments, sex and drugs—so that they felt that they were thinking. "Slippery stuff", like philosophy and sociology, was avoided, for it led to melancholy.

Beatty rose to leave, reminding Montag of his duty to stem the "torrent of melancholy and dreary philosophy." Before he left, he observed that at least once in his career a fireman had the urge to read one of the books he was supposed to burn. However, he declared, books had nothing to say. Consequently, a fireman was allowed to keep the book for twenty-four hours. If it had not been returned by then, the firemen simply came to burn it for him.

As Beatty left, Montag told him that he would perhaps come in for his shift later. But in his own mind Montag had resolved never to return to his work.

p. 57 *"Montag watched through the window . . ."*

As Montag watched Beatty drive away, he glanced at the houses in the street. He was reminded of Clarisse's observation that the houses had no front porches. For front porches encouraged people to talk together too much. Gardens and rocking-chairs had gone for the same reason. In the words of Clarisse's uncle, the modern idea was to "Get people up and running around."

p. 58 *"Montag turned and looked at his wife . . ."*

As Montag turned to his wife, she was engrossed in the parlor walls. He told her that he felt destructive, but her only comment was that he should take the beetle for a drive, since she always went for a drive at ninety-five miles an hour when she felt like that. Montag insisted that in spite of knowing that "Fun is everything", he was not happy. When Mildred persisted in concentrating her attention on the parlor walls, Montag switched off the sound and declared that he wanted her to see something that he had been hiding for the past year. He went to the air-conditioning grille in the hall and pulled out twenty books. Mildred shrank away from them in horror. Finally, she seized one and attempted to throw it into the incinerator, but Montag prevented her. He pleaded with her to take time with him to read the books, so that they could decide whether Beatty was right. He reminded her of the old woman who had been burnt with her books, and declared that Beatty had seemed to be afraid of her. At any rate, he had come to the conclusion that he did not like the firemen nor himself.

Montag was interrupted by a voice softly calling at the door. In spite of his fear, he persuaded Mildred to ignore the sound until, at last, the caller went away.

Montag took up a book and began reading. Mildred protested when he read something aloud that it did not mean anything, that Beatty was right. But with grim determination, Montag said that they must start at the beginning.

PART TWO: THE SIEVE AND THE SAND

p. 63   *"They read the long afternoon through . . ."*

While Mildred stared blankly at the silent parlour walls, Montag read all afternoon. He became frustrated. One book wrote of the beginning of friendship, which he thought he must have experienced with Clarisse. Another began with its author's 'favourite topic', Myself, which—strangely—Mildred said she understood. However, Montag was puzzled because Clarisse's favourite subject had not been herself, but others.

Their reading was interrupted momentarily by a sound at the door. Montag froze at the "smell of blue electricity blowing under the locked door", though Mildred assured him that it was only a dog.

Mildred objected to their reading, finding in the books nothing to compare with the cheerful company of her "family" on the parlor walls, and being horrified at the thought that the house and their "family" might be burned as punishment. Montag brushed her objections aside, declaring that they should read because of the Snake that had emptied her stomach and of the old woman burned with her books and of Clarisse McClellan who lay in the morgue. The sound of the ever-present bombers overhead made him ask questions about his society: why no one explained the presence of the bombers; why they were there in spite of winning two atomic wars since 1960; why there might be truth in the rumours that their society is hated by the rest of the world.

As Mildred answered a telephone call from Ann, who was enquiring about a television program that evening, Montag realized that his task was hopeless without a teacher, for he could not understand the books. Suddenly he thought of the old man he had met in the park a year before. His name was Faber, a retired English Professor who had lost his job forty years ago when the last liberal arts college had closed for lack of students and patronage. He had talked to Montag for over an hour, not of things, but of the meaning of things. Faber had given Montag his address in case, he observed wryly, the fireman decided to be angry with him. Surprised at himself, Montag had assured Faber that he was not angry.

p. 67 *"Mildred shrieked with laughter . . ."*

As Mildred talked on the telephone, Montag, after consulting his file, called Faber on another telephone. He asked the professor how many copies were left of the Bible, of Shakespeare and of Plato Fearing a trap, Faber hung up after stating that Montag knew that there were none left.

With excitement, Montag showed Mildred one of the books, declaring it might be the last copy of the Bible in existence. Mildred replied that it did not matter, since he had to give it to Beatty that night. Montag pointed out that he did not know which book Beatty believed him to possess. In answer, Mildred began to scream, claiming that Montag was going to ruin them. Montag could hear, then, in his mind the menacing voice of Beatty talking lovingly of the burning book. Consequently, Montag, not listening to his now-silent wife, decided that he must have a copy of the book made that night before it had to be given to Beatty.

As Montag was leaving the house, Mildred, distressed, asked him if he would be back in time to watch the White Clown on television, for her women friends would be visiting. Montag turned and asked Mildred if the White Clown and all her "family" loved her. She dismissed his question as being silly, and Montag felt as though he wanted to cry, though he could not.

Mildred asked him to kick the dog outside, if it were still there. Her remark caused him to open the door and step out cautiously. With a sigh of relief, he found the street to be empty. He slammed the door behind him.

p. 69 *"He was on the subway."*

On the subway, Montag reflected that he was numb, with a numbness he thought had begun the night he had kicked the pill-bottle. But the numbness would be taken away by Faber or by someone else, who would give him back "the old face and the old hands the way they were." Even the "burnt-in smile" was gone now, and he felt lost without it.

He recalled that as a child, sitting on a sand-dune by the sea, a cruel cousin had promised him a dime for filling a sieve with sand. The faster he had poured, the faster the sieve emptied, until tears had coursed down his cheeks. Now, as he clutched the open Bible in his hand, the "terrible logic" of that sieve came back to him, but—he thought—perhaps with reading some of the sand stayed in the sieve. But in a few hours, there would be Beatty. Montag clenched the book in his hands, willing himself to remember what he read.

As he tried to hold in his mind a passage from the Sermon on the Mount, his thoughts were interrupted by the rhythmic, insistent sound of the train radio advertising Denham's Dentifrice. His mind in torment, Montag found himself on his feet, screaming for the sound of the radio to stop. The other people stared and voiced objections. When the train stopped at Knoll View station, he hurled himself from the train, wanting only to feel his body in motion. The sound of the train radio floated after him as the train hissed like a snake and disappeared.

p. 71 *"Who is it?"*

Faber was reluctant to open his door to Montag, being fearful until he saw the book the fireman carried. He declared that Montag was a brave man for having stolen the book he carried, but Montag responded that he was not brave. He wanted help, because his wife was dying, a friend had already died, and someone who might have been a friend had been burnt twenty-four hours before.

Although not a religious man, Faber examined the Bible lovingly. He concluded that it was just as good as he remembered it, in contrast with the figure of Christ on the parlor walls, where He was now "a regular peppermint stick . . . all sugar-crystal and saccharine when he isn't making veiled references to certain commercial products that every worshiper *absolutely* needs." Even the smell of the book attracted him, for all books smelled like nutmeg or some foreign spice. Contemplating the book, Faber confessed that he was a coward, because he had seen what was happening and had said nothing. Now it was too late.

Faber asked why Montag had come to see him. The fireman replied that he needed someone to talk to, in the hope that he would be able to understand what he read. He did not know what had happened to him; he thought that books might help. Faber retorted that Montag was a hopeless romantic, and that it was not books he needed. He really needed some of the things that were once in books. Old phonograph records, old movies and old friends could supply the "infinite detail and awareness" he yearned for; even the parlor walls could be made to do that. Books were simply one kind of receptacle that had been used to store things that men were afraid they would forget. Thus, the only "magic" in books was in the way in which they "stitched the patches of the universe into one garment for us."

Three things were missing for Montag, according to Faber. The first was quality of information, which meant fresh and telling detail. Books like the Bible were important because they revealed "truthfully recorded details of life." In Faber's words, "The good writers touch life often." That was why books were hated and feared. Good books had features; modern society preferred the featureless. Unfortunately, then, that society was like the ancient wrestler Antaeus, who was invincible when he had his feet planted firmly on the ground, but was defeated by Hercules, who held him in midair. That legend applied to the city. The second requirement, in Faber's view, was leisure. That did not mean simply "off-hours" to be filled in by insistent, overpowering parlor walls, but real leisure to digest the quality of information. Finally, what was required was the right to act on the quality information which had been digested at leisure. But Faber thought it too late for an old man and "a fireman turned sour" to do anything about that.

Montag suggested that he could obtain books, and that Faber and he could print extra copies of them. Faber rejected the suggestion, declaring that he would only take part in such a plan if there were no risk of getting burnt. Jokingly, he continued, they might first destroy the firemen by planting extra copies of books in their houses. Montag stated that he was willing to give the scheme a try, if Faber promised that it would help. However, the professor informed the fireman that he was wrong in seeking such guarantees. The only way was to do one's own "bit of saving."

Nevertheless, the idea intrigued Faber. There were old professors and former actors who might participate. They might also form classes in thinking and reading. But still, Faber insisted, the task was hopeless, because the whole culture was affected. The only hope was for the war to blow the world to pieces. He advised Montag to go home.

As Montag prepared to leave. First, he offered the Bible to Faber. When he expressed his great desire to have the book, Montag began

24

to rip out the pages, much to Faber's agony. He stopped only when the professor agreed to help him.

Faber asked Montag to bring the four or five hundred dollars he had. The professor knew an unemployed printer. They could start a few books and wait for the outbreak of war, during which their "stage-whisper" might be heard.

Again preparing to go, Montag asked Faber for help in talking to Captain Beatty, who has "read enough so he has all the answers." In response, Faber took Montag into the bedroom, where he showed him a collection of electronic equipment. This, declared Faber, was the result of his "terrible cowardice." His fear had led him to design a tiny radio transmitter which fitted into the ear. For years he had waited in his fear for someone with whom he could exchange messages. Now he instructed Montag to insert the device in his ear and to go to the firehouse. They would then be able to listen to Beatty together, and Faber would send messages to Montag. Finally, Faber promised to see the printer the next day.

Montag left, emerging into the dark street and looking at the world.

p. 82 *"You could feel the war . . ."*

Outside, the night felt as though war were imminent, for the stars "looked, a million of them swimming between the clouds, like the enemy discs."

Montag had visited the all-night bank to withdraw the money for the printer. As the Seashell radio in his ear brought news of war preparations, Faber's voice cut in. Montag protested that he had not really changed: he was still just doing what he was told, and not thinking for himself. He wanted to know when he could start working things out on his own; he did not simply want to change sides and still be told what to do. However, Faber assured him that by talking like that he was already showing his new wisdom. As Montag walked to his house, Faber began reading aloud to him from the Book of Job.

p. 83 *"He was eating . . ."*

At nine o'clock, as he was eating supper, Mrs. Phelps and Mrs. Bowles arrived. Mildred rushed to greet them. The three disappeared into the parlor, adding their loud conversation to the din of the parlor walls.

Montag stood at the parlor door, listening to the inane comments of the women as they watched television. He whispered almost to himself that he should be on his way to Faber with the money, but the professor's voice assured him that to-morrow was time enough.

The women watched ecstatically as the parlor walls showed a drink of orange juice coursing its way to a woman's stomach, a rocket plunging through air and ocean, and jet cars crashing into one another with bodies flying through the air.

Montag shut off the switch to the parlor walls. The women turned to look at Montag with irritation and dislike. He asked them abruptly when they thought the war would start, since he had noticed that their husbands were not with them. Mrs. Phelps replied that the Army had called her husband yesterday, but that he would be back next week. The war was expected to be a quick one, only forty-eight hours. As the three women fidgeted and looked nervously at the blank parlor walls, she went on to say that in any case she was not worried. She would let her husband do the worrying; at any rate, it was always someone else's husband who died. Mildred added that she had never known anyone to be killed in war; sove died by jumping off a building—like Gloria's husband, last week—but not in war. Furthermore, Mrs. Phelps concluded, her husband and she had decided that there would be no tears over one another; this was third marriage for both of them, and if he died she was simply to get married again, with no tears. Mildred took up the conversation again by discussing the five-minute romance she had seen on television last night.

Montag was silent as he looked at the women. Once, as a child, he had entered a strange church and looked at the faces of the statue saints. In spite of his "trying to know what religion was", the enameled faces of the saints had meant nothing to him. It had been like being in a strange store in which his money was unusable. So it was now with these women. As he stared at them, the tension in the room grew until at last he suggested that they talk.

He began by asking Mrs. Phelps how her children were, but she retorted that no one in his right mind would have children. However, Mrs. Bowles declared that she had had two children, both by Caesarian section since she did not want to suffer any pain. The children were no bother; they were in school nine days out of ten, and when they were at home she simply threw them into the parlor and turned on television. Her friends laughed as she observed: "They'd just as soon kick as kiss me. Thank God, I can kick back!"

Mildred, to please Guy, suggested that they discuss politics. Mrs. Bowles stated that she had voted in the last election for President Noble, "one of the nicest looking men." The women agreed that he was much better than the man the "Outs" had run, Hubert Hoag, who was "small and homely", was too fat, and had picked his nose on television. The discussion ended with Mildred asking Montag to go away and stop making them nervous.

He left the room, but returned with a book in his hand. Faber began to plead with him in whispers not to do anything foolish, but Montag angrily dismissed the professor's objections, uttering his disgust for the women, whom he described as "monsters talking about monsters." The three women were nervous and upset, and Montag made them sit before him. Mrs. Phelps, trying to placate him, suggested that he read a nice poem from the book; Mrs. Bowles wailed that that would not be right. Mildred, upset by her husband's wild conversation with someone she could not see, tried to smooth over the situation by saying that once a year every fireman was allowed to bring a book home to show his family how silly it was; she suggested that Montag read some of the "junk" so that they would not have to bother their heads with it again.

In a low, stumbling voice, Montag read Matthew Arnold's *Dover Beach*. When he had finished, Mrs. Phelps was crying uncontrollably. Mrs. Bowles condemned Montag for upsetting them with that "mush", and Montag dropped the book into the incinerator. Mildred tried to calm her friends, but Mrs. Bowles stated that she would never visit "this crazy fireman's house again." In turn, Montag fixed his eyes upon her and told her to go home in order to think of her two dead husbands, her dozen abortions and of her children who hated her. The women left, slamming the door behind them.

As Mildred ran to the bathroom to take her pills, Montag snatched the radio transmitter from his ear, for Faber was condemning his actions. He went quickly through the house, gathering up his books. He took them out into the garden and hid them in the bushes near the alley fence. When he returned to the house, Mildred did not answer when he called her name.

On his way to the fire station, Montag re-inserted the radio in his ear. Now, he knew, he was two people, Montag and Faber, but in time a new Montag would emerge under the tutelage of Faber. Out of two separate and opposite things would emerge the new person. He felt as though he were undertaking a long journey, "the going-away from the self he had been."

As Montag approached the fire-house, Faber calmed and cajoled him. Montag's feet felt frozen with uncertainty, for he was afraid of making the same mistake with Beatty as he had with the women at home. Survival, Faber urged, must be Montag's objective.

In the fire-house, the Mechanical Hound was gone, and the

Salamander stood silent. Beatty welcomed him, asking at once for the book, and declaring that he hoped Montag had returned to stay with them. As they sat and played cards, Montag felt his guilt strongly, conscious that his hands had committed wrong. Thus, twice in half an hour, he had to go to the washroom.

Beatty proceeded to create in Montag a feeling of panic by quoting to him confusing and paradoxical statements from literature, until Montag's head "whirled sickeningly." All through Beatty's harangue, Faber's voice whispered to Montag, urging him to keep calm and to restrain himself. At the end of it, Montag sat "like a carved white stone." Faber tried to reassure him, by saying that Montag must digest all that had been said and then make up his mind carefully himself. Montag was just about to make the error of replying to Faber when the alarm voice interrupted with a call.

Beatty seemed to be in no hurry to respond to the alarm, walking with "exaggerated slowness." At first he said that they would finish the game of cards. Then he expressed concern that Montag was not well. Finally, since they had been called to a "special case", he decided that they should leave.

As they drove, Montag felt anger, anger at his reading to the women in his parlor, for his action now seemed like "trying to put out fires with waterpistols." He was jolted from his reverie by the voice of Beatty, who was driving, though he usually did not do so. The Captain was smiling furiously, and cried out: "Here we go to keep the world happy, Montag!"

When they came to a halt, Montag felt that he could not take part in another fire. Then, with astonishment, he realized that they had stopped in front of his house.

PART THREE: BURNING BRIGHT

p. 100 *"Lights flicked on . . ."*

The neighbours gathered to watch the firemen set up their equipment for destruction, as Beatty and Montag looked on, the former with satisfaction, the latter with disbelief. Beatty asked Montag why he had not taken the hint when the Hound had been sent round to his door, but Montag could only look numbly to the house next door. As he saw this, Beatty expressed his scorn that Montag had been led astray by Clarisse's talk.

Mildred emerged from the house, "her body stiff, her face floured with powder, her mouth gone, without lipstick." Her waiting beetle shot her away as she mumbled incoherently about the loss of her "family", with Montag asking incredulously whether she had turned in the alarm.

As Stoneman and Black smashed the windows of the house, Montag contacted Faber, who asked him whether he could escape. Meanwhile, Beatty relished the flame of his igniter, declaring that the "clean, quick, sure" fire would lift the burden of Montag from his shoulders. All during this, Montag gazed numbly at the house, with its broken windows and ripped books lying on the floor, books that now "looked silly." Watching, he realized that Mildred had brought the books he had hidden back from the garden.

In reply to Faber's urgent questioning, Montag responded that he could not escape because of the Hound. Beatty, hearing the answer, confirmed the presence of the Hound in the neighbourhood, and instructed Montag to set fire to the books. Montag directed the spout of fire with relish, destroying the bedroom which he had shared with a "strange" woman, burning the "vacuum" of the parlor. "Fire," he thought, "was best for everything!"

Beatty informed him that when he was finished he was under arrest.

p. 103 *"The house fell . . ."*

At three-thirty in the morning, the house fell in and the neighbours returned home, Montag, sooty and drenched in perspiration, tried to speak twice, and finally was able to ask whether Mildred had indeed turned in the alarm. Beatty revealed that she had, though her friends had also done so earlier. Montag's action in reading poetry, the Captain declared, had been foolish.

Montag could not move. It was as though an earthquake had engulfed his house, burying his "entire life." And now the earthquake was inside him. Tired, bewildered and outraged, he heard Beatty ask why he had done this. At the same moment, Faber's voice cut in, urging escape. Finally, Beatty struck him, sending the transmitter hurtling from his ear. The Captain pounced upon the instrument, promising that they would track down Montag's friend. At this, Montag switched on the flame-thrower. Beatty at first started with surprise, then defied Montag's threat scornfully. As he walked toward the fireman, Montag directed the flame at him. Beatty became a "gibbering mannikin" engulfed in liquid fire. When Beatty lay still, Montag aimed the flame-thrower at Stoneman and Black and knocked them unconscious with a blow as they turned their backs in response to his order.

Then the Mechanical Hound arrived. As it leaped at him, Montag directed the flame upon it. The fire "snapped the hound up in the air" and "blew out its interior", but not before it had thrust its procaine needle into Montag's leg. Painfully and with difficulty, Montag escaped into the darkness to the accompaniment of shouts. Stumbling along the dark alley, he thought grimly that he had obeyed Beatty's instructions not to face a problem, but to burn it.

p. 107 *"A shotgun blast went off . . ."*

Montag cursed himself as he limped off painfully. He had been a fool; he had tried to do everything at once. He was tempted to give himself up, but rejected the thought, for if he had to burn he would take a few more with him. Then he remembered the books. He returned to the garden and found four that Mildred had missed.

Escaping with them, he was suddenly halted and paralyzed by a stunning realization: Beatty had wanted to die. The Captain had seemed deliberately to enrage Montag, until Montag's action had been inevitable. Montag was nauseated as he thought of Beatty's death, for the fireman had not wanted to kill anyone, and he muttered his regrets.

At the sound of pursuing footsteps, he arose agonizingly. At first, the pains were like "spikes driven in the kneecap", but gradually his leg began to feel more normal. Running, he thought of Faber, realizing that the man was safe now, because the transmitter had been burned with Beatty. Grimly, he reflected that the advice, "burn them or they'll burn you", did simplify matters.

He felt in his pockets, discovering that he still had the money drawn earlier from the bank, and a Seashell radio. Already his name was being broadcast on a police alert. Montag came to a ten-lane highway, which he felt was too broad to cross safely. Directly ahead, he noticed a gas station. This would enable him to clean up and so appear more normal before escaping. But then he realized that he had nowhere to go—except to Faber. Faber could not hide him. He had to see Faber, just to know that "there was a man like Faber in the world." He could also leave Faber money. After that, he could perhaps head for the open country.

Looking overhead, Montag saw two dozen police helicopters in the sky. They settled occasionally in the streets where, turned into beetles, they searched for the fugitive.

p. 111 *"And here was the gas station . . ."*

Approaching the gas station from the rear, Montag entered the men's room and washed. While he was doing so, he heard a radio announcement that war had been declared. It seemed to have no effect on the people outside, and Montag was surprised that it did not affect him greatly.

Outside, Montag once more faced the highway, which seemed to lie like "a game for him to win." Ignoring the headlights of a car three blocks away, he began to cross. He started to run as the beetle picked up speed and rushed towards him. He reached the half-way point, but he could hear the engines whining higher. It was the police, he thought, and he forced himself to walk so as not to seem concerned. However, the beetle picked up speed, reaching 130 m.p.h. at least. Montag broke into a run, dropping one of his books. Just as the car seemed to be almost on top of him, he stumbled and fell. The fall saved him, for the car swerved and disappeared. Montag heard wisps of laughter as it went, and he realized that it had missed him by no more than one-sixteenth of an inch. It had not been a police car, but only a carful of children playing a deadly game. They had not identified him as the wanted fugitive, but had simply been attracted by the rare sight of a man strolling. They would have killed him for no reason at all. As he stumbled on, his books back in his hands, he wondered whether those children had killed Clarisse. Montag gasped at the thought of his near escape. However, four blocks away the car turned and began to race back. Montag quickly escaped into the darkness.

Overhead, the helicopters still continued their search, falling intermittently from the sky "like the first flakes of snow in the long winter to come . . ."

p. 115 *"The house was silent."*

Montag stopped at Black's house, which stood silent. He entered by the back door, assuming that Mrs. Black was asleep, and hid his books in the kitchen. On his way across town, he phoned in a fire alarm, and stood waiting for the firemen to come to burn Mr. Black's house.

p. 115 *"Faber!"*

At Faber's house, Montag told Faber what had happened. Montag wondered aloud how so much had happened to him in a single week, but Faber assured him that it had all been "coming on" for a long time. Montag agreed, since he confessed that for a long time he had been going around doing one thing and feeling another.

Montag expressed anxiety that he might have been followed, but Faber declared that his own fear had gone, for at last he felt that he was doing the right thing. When Faber continued by asking Montag's plans, Montag replied that he was going to keep on running. He gave Faber one hundred dollars to use for their earlier plan. Faber advised him to head for the river. By following it, he could reach the railroad tracks, now disused, which led out into the country. He had heard that there were still hobo camps all across the country and even "lots of old Harvard degrees on the tracks between here and Los Angeles." Montag might be able to hide and then get in touch with Faber in St. Louis. Faber declared that he was coming out of hiding at last and would travel to St. Louis that morning to see a retired printer.

Before Montag left, the men watched a small television set in Faber's bedroom. It carried news of the search for Montag, with the ominous information that a new Mechanical Hound had been brought into the district and that the television camera was going to follow the Hound in its pursuit. Faber showed fear as they watched the Hound being unloaded at the site of Montag's burned house. Montag almost wished that he could savour and enjoy the search on television, being confronted at the last moment with an audience of twenty or thirty million.

However, Montag urged Faber to destroy all traces of his visitor's presence and to kill the scent by turning on the garden sprinklers. Faber gave him a valise of old clothes, dousing the exterior with whiskey in order to kill the scent of Faber. Promising to contact Faber in St. Louis, Montag ran off through the spray of the lawn sprinklers.

p. 121 *"Montag ran."*

As Montag ran, he could feel the silent pressure of the Hound somewhere behind him. He peered through the window of a house and watched the chase on television. The Hound reached Faber's house, stopped indecisively, and then plunged away again. With an effort, Montag pushed himself away from the window.

As he ran, he jammed his Seashell radio into his ear. He heard the police order all citizens in the area to open their doors and look into the streets for the fugitive. At the count of ten, all of the doors opened, but Montag had reached the river.

He tossed aside his own clothes and dressed in the garments Faber had given him. Then he entered the water.

p. 124 *"He was three hundred yards downstream . . ."*

When Montag was three hundred yards downstream, the Hound reached the river. Searchlights bathed the water, and Montag dived under to escape their light. Then the helicopters swerved over the city as though they had picked up a new trail, and the Hound went away. There was sudden peacefulness, and Montag felt he was "moving from an unreality that was frightening into a reality that unreal because it was new."

Floating on the river, Montag reflected on the stars, the moon and the burning sun. The sun would not stop burning, but men had to. "Somewhere the saving and putting away had to begin again . . ."

As the river current brought him to land, he was hesitant, fearing that the silent trees might "blow under a great wind of helicopters." But there was only silence, and he wondered how Millie would react to that silence. However, no one was there. The dry smell of hay blown from a distant field reminded him of a farm he had visited when he was very young. He thought of sleeping in a barn all night and gazing from the loft window upon a young girl from long ago who knew what it meant when dandelions rubbed off on your chin. And in the morning he would awake refreshed to a gift of fresh milk and fresh fruit.

As he stepped from the river, the land seemed to rush at him, for it seemed like too much land. It swam, like that day in his childhood, until he felt nauseated.

Suddenly, Montag heard a whisper which he thought was the Hound. But it was only a nervous deer. Montag exulted in the leaves under his feet and the smell of the land all round him. He stood, breathing and being filled by the land.

As he moved, his foot encountered the disused railroad track. This was his road. As he walked, he was certain of one fact that he could not prove—that Clarisse had walked where he was now walking.

p. 129 *"Half an hour later . . ."*

Half an hour later Montag saw a fire. This was a fire different from what he had known. It was a warming fire, round which a group of men sat, now meditatively silent, now easily conversing about many different things.

One of the five old men sitting round the fire, bearded and dressed in dark blue denim pants and jackets and dark blue shirts, welcomed him. Montag was given hot coffee and a potion which would change the smell of his perspiration in order to confuse the Hound.

The men knew Montag because they had watched the hunt on television. The set was switched on again and they watched the chase. The leader of the men, Granger, explained that they would be able to watch the capture of Montag. The police would not admit defeat; they would seek a scapegoat. He would be someone who had been observed to have unusual habits, such as that of walking the streets in the early hours because of insomnia. The telecast proved the truth of Granger's words. The Hound pounced upon an innocent victim, and an announcer declared that the crime against society had been avenged with the death of Montag.

Granger welcomed Montag back from the dead and introduced his companions: Fred Clement, a former professor of literature at Cambridge, Dr. Simmons, a specialist in Spanish literature from U.C.L.A., Professor West, a professor of ethics from Columbia University, and Reverend Padover, a former minister. Granger revealed that he himself had written a book on the relationship between the individual and society. In reply, Montag said that he had been such a fool that he did not belong with them. However, Granger replied that they had all made the right kind of mistakes, and he asked what Montag had to offer. Ruefully, Montag said that he had had part of the *Book of Ecclesiastes* and a little of *Revelation*, but only in his memory. Granger welcomed that statement, for he revealed that they all memorized books, having trained their memories. Only one man, Harris in Youngstown, was, through memory, the *Book of Ecclesiastes*. Therefore, Montag was valuable. Moreover, Montag was told that Granger was Plato's *Republic*, Simmons was Marcus Aurelius, another Jonathan Swift, another Charles Darwin, another Schopenhauer, another Einstein, another Albert Schweitzer, and still others were various writers and philosophers.

Montag was incredulous. But Granger assured him that they had found memory to be the safest technique, since they had to travel so much. Thus, Montag declared that he had been foolish in wanting to plant books in the houses of firemen. However, Granger commented that the idea was a good one, if carried out on a national scale. But their idea was better. They simply wanted to preserve knowledge. Thus they did not seek to incite anyone; they were waiting for the war to begin and end quickly, so that afterwards they might be of some use. Some day, he continued, even if they had to wait to pass the knowledge on to their children, they would be useful. For, Granger revealed, there were thousands of them, and when they were needed they would appear to recite their knowledge so that books could be printed. That might last only until another Dark Age. However, he declared, "that's the wonderful thing about man; he never gets so discouraged or disgusted that he gives up doing it all over again, because he knows very well it is important and *worth* the doing."

They put out the fire, in preparation for moving downstream.

34

p. 137 *"They stood by the river in the starlight."*

Montag asked why they trusted him. He was told that his appearance—*"you* look like hell"—was sufficient! In addition, the cities did not usually bother them, for to the cities they were only "a few crackpots with verses in their heads."

Montag looked with wonderment at his companions. He had expected to see the light of "a triumph over tomorrow" in their faces, but they looked no different from any others. Moreover, they did not seem to be certain that what they carried in their memories "might make every future dawn glow with a purer light." They laughed off Montag's puzzlement by advising him not to judge a book by its cover.

p. 138 *"There was a shriek . . ."*

To the sound of jets overhead, Montag looked back at the city and, self-reproachfully, observed that he did not miss Millie, nor would he even feel sad if she died. Granger took his arm and told Montag about his grandfather, who had been a sculptor. Granger had cried when the old man had died, and he had never gotten over the old man's death. But the tears had been for what the old man had done and been. The grief was caused by the realization that "The world was bankrupted of ten million fine actions the night he passed on." Montag replied that he could think of nothing when he thought of Mildred, for the city had given him nothing but ashes, and in the city people gave one another nothingness.

Granger revealed that his grandfather had said that everyone left something behind when he died. It did not matter what one did, but only that "you change something from the way it was before you touched it into something that's like you after you take your hands away." The old man, Granger continued, had shown him some V-2 rocket films fifty years ago. From two hundred miles in the air, their atomic mushroom had seemed like a pin-prick. Nature, in contrast, was vast, and man needed it to show himself how small he really was. Man had to see the world, which is "more fantastic than any dream made or paid for in factories."

Suddenly the war interrupted their conversation. It began and ended in an instant as the bombers, flying at five thousand miles an hour, destroyed the city. Montag knew in that moment that Faber's bus would be travelling only to another scene of desolation. He imagined Millie's empty face at the moment of her death. And then he remembered that it was in Chicago that he and Millie had met. As he pressed himself to the earth, Montag saw the city flung into the air.

p. 143 *"Montag, lying there . . ."*

As he clutched the earth, gasping and crying, Montag found himself able to recall part of the *Book of Ecclesiastes*. All around him, the other men were holding onto the earth grimly, shouting aloud against the air pressure on their eardrums. In the midst of the noise, Montag vowed to see the world, so that he could make it part of his blood.

The wind died and, after a pause, the men rose. The city had gone, and Montag wondered how many other cities had died. As the sun rose, the men lit a fire and prepared breakfast, before starting upstream, towards the city. Watching the fire, Granger mentioned the Phoenix, the mythical bird which sprang to life again every time it was burned to ashes. Man, he reflected, was like the Phoenix. But, he continued, man was different in that he knew the silly things he was doing. Thus, "some day we'll stop making the goddam funeral pyres and jumping in the middle of them."

Before they left, Granger urged them to remember that they were not important in themselves, but that what they carried in their memories might help. That was not certain, since when the world had books it had not heeded them. Now, when they met lonely people their only task was to declare that they were remembering. Then one day they would win out. Right now, they had to build a mirror factory and take a long look into the mirrors.

As they walked back to the city, the men were silent because "there was everything to think about and much to remember." They were no doubt, Montag reflected, thinking of what they would have to say when it came to their turn to speak from their memories. He, recalling *Revelation*, knew what he would say:

> "And on either side of the river was there a tree of life, which bare twelve manner of fruits, and yielded her fruit every month; And the leaves of the tree were for the healing of nations.

He would save those words for noon, when they reached the city.

CHARACTER OUTLINES

(in the order of their appearance in the novel)

GUY MONTAG

Guy Montag, a fireman employed by the state at a salary of about six thousand dollars a year, is a man whose true nature unfolds and develops as the novel progresses. At first, he seems to be a man who is absorbed in his work. Thus the novel opens—startlingly—with the expression of his delight in his job: "It was a pleasure to burn." Moreover, he seems to look forward with pleasurable satisfaction to the end of a good day's work:

> He knew that when he returned to the firehouse, he might wink at himself, a minstrel-man, burnt-corked, in the mirror. Later, going to sleep, he would feel the fiery smile still gripped by his face muscles, in the dark. It never went away, that smile, it never ever went away, as long as he remembered. (pp.3-4)

However, even at the very beginning of the book, there are indications that either Montag is not nearly so suited for his work as he would seem to be, or that there is another, hidden aspect of his personality which his devotion to burning conceals. For example, it is worthwhile to examine closely his description of the joy of burning, on the first page:

> It was a special pleasure to see things eaten, to see things blackened and *changed*. With the brass nozzle in his fists, with this great python spitting its venomous kerosene upon the world, the blood pounded in his head, and his hands were the hands of some amazing conductor playing all the symphonies of blazing and burning to bring down the tatters and charcoal ruins of history. With his symbolic helmet numbered 451 on his stolid head, and his eyes all orange flame with the thought of what came next, he flicked the igniter and the house jumped up in a gorging fire that burned the evening sky red and yellow and black. He strode in a swarm of fireflies.

A number of important observations can be made about this passage. In the first place, it is impressive for the poetic romanticism with which the task of burning is described. As Montag conceives himself to be a kind of *maestro* conducting a symphony of burning, the mood is emphatically lyrical. Ugly reality is absent, and thus, in effect, the passage makes one wonder at the appropriateness of having such a romantic soul engaged in such a destructive task. In this way, the first stirrings of doubt raised by the apparent contrast between the character and his work might be discerned. Further, in the passage there is obviously an absence of reference to human beings in the act of burning. Things are being burned, but there is no reference to possible human suffering and anguish in the situation. The "tatters and charcoal ruins of history" are being brought down, but there is no cry of human destruction. Again a question might be raised as to how this character might react if human agony came to be involved in what he was doing. Finally, the fireman's description of his firehose is worth noting; it is a "great python spitting its venomous kerosene upon the world." The metaphor hardly attributes favourable connotations to the act of burning. The snake is an ancient symbol of evil. Thus, in some way Montag perceives the evil, destructive nature of his task. Obviously, then, it would be a mistake to be unaware, even very early in the novel, of aspects of the character of Montag which show him to be less than content with his lot. It would be a mistake to trust entirely the picture of Montag as being a carefree individual completely happy in his work, who is able to leave his day's destruction whistling merrily (p. 4).

Montag suffers from a kind of spiritual schizophrenia. There are within him two selves which struggle for supremacy. Like Brutus in *Julius Caesar*, he knows the experience of a war taking place within the self:

> Between the acting of a dreadful thing
> And the first motion, all the interim is
> Like a phantasma, or a hideous dream:
> The Genius and the mortal instruments
> Are then in council; and the state of man,
> Like to a little kingdom, suffers then
> The nature of an insurrection.   (Act II, scene 1, lines 63-69)

In a sense, *Fahrenheit 451* is Montag's struggle with the "hideous dream", is the account of the war between Montag's training and Montag's nature. His mind suffers, as it were, civil war, fought between his role as a fireman and his inclinations as a person. In the early stages of the novel, he is obviously experiencing only the first skirmishes in that conflict, and his understanding is not complete. Thus, he talks to "that other self", knowing it only as "the subconscious idiot that ran babbling at times, quite independent of will, habit, and conscience" (p. 10). His awareness of his divided self is at first only an awareness that his apparent happiness is only a pose: "He wore his happiness like a mask . . ." (p. 11). His awareness is limited to feeling rather than understanding, to emotion rather than to thought:

> He felt his body divide itself into a hotness and a coldness, a softness and a hardness, a trembling and a not trembling, the two halves grinding one upon the other.   (p. 22)

Later, however, he arrives at understanding. Before his final encounter with Beatty at the station, Montag reflects on himself and on
his relationship with Faber, and declares:

> . . . Now, he knew that he was two people, that he was, above all,
> Montag who knew nothing, who did not even know himself a fool, but
> only suspected it. And he knew that he was also the old man who
> talked to him and talked to him as the train was sucked from one end
> of the night city to the other on one long sickening gasp of motion. In
> the days to follow, and in the nights when there was no moon and in
> the nights when there was a very bright moon shining on the earth, the
> old man would go on with this talking and talking, drop by drop, stone
> by stone, flake by flake. His mind would well over at last and he would
> not be Montag any more, this the old man told him, assured him,
> promised him. He would be Montag-plus-Faber, fire plus water, and
> then, one day, after everything had mixed and simmered and worked
> away in silence, there would be neither fire nor water,, but wine. Out
> of two separate and opposite things, a third. And one day he would
> look back upon the fool and know the fool. Even now he could feel
> the start of the long journey, the leave-taking, the going-away from the
> self he had been.   (p. 93)

The plot of the novel, then, involves the resolution of the inner
conflict which creates in Montag only a vague feeling of uneasiness at
the outset.

That Montag is a person who suffers the tension of a divided self is
inevitable in view of other aspects of his character. He is, for
example, obviously a person of warm humanity, with feelings of
compassion for his fellow human beings. A year before the novel
begins, he has met Faber on a park-bench. Even though their meeting
had been "strange" and "Quiet" had in fact been no more than "an
hour of monologue, a poem, a comment" (pp. 66-67), Faber had been
able to reach the warm, human feelings within Montag, so that the
fireman had not reported the old man. Indeed, such was Montag's
own limited understanding of himself at the time, that he had been
surprised to find that he was not angry with the old man. The same
basic warmth of nature is evident in the conversation with Clarisse
(pp. 26ff). Clarisse realizes that Montag loves children; his marriage is
childless because Mildred "just never wanted any children at all".
The same sensitivity is illustrated in Montag's reaction to the process
that follows Mildred's taking an overdose of sleeping tablets (p. 12ff).
His marriage is hardly fulfilling, and his relationship with his wife is
impersonal. For example, when he arrives home (pp. 10-11) the
bedroom seems like "the cold marbled room of a mausoleum", and
he pictures Mildred stretched out of the bed, "like a body displayed
on the lid of a tomb." Such is the relationship between Montag and

Mildred that neither can remember when they first met! However, Montag's sensitivity is nonetheless offended by the crisis of her illness. The operators who arrive to treat her offend Montag by their lack of personal interest in the woman they are helping. Thus, the woman on the bed "was no more than a hard stratum of marble they reached." The whole operation was "not unlike the digging of a trench in one's yard." The attitude of the technicians is well exemplified by their description of their task:

> "Got to clean 'em out both ways," said the operator, standing over the silent woman. "No use getting the stomach if you don't clean the blood. Leave that stuff in the blood and the blood hits the brain like a mallet, bang, a couple thousand mes, and the brain just gives up, just quits." (pp. 13-14)

As a result, Montag's sensibilities are so offended that he orders the technician to be quiet. When the operators leave, Montag is left to reflect on the lack of humanity in the entire proceedings:

> . . . Nobody knows anyone. Strangers come and violate you. Strangers come and cut your heart out. Strangers come and take your blood. Good God, who *were* those men? I never saw them before in my *life*!
> (p. 15)

Montag's sensitivity is disturbed by the same lack of the personal element in his marriage. That is why it is so important to him that they should remember when Mildred and he first met (p. 39); and that is why he is appalled by the thought that he would not cry, even if she died:

> . . . he remembered thinking then that if she died, he was certain he wouldn't cry. For it would be the dying of an unknown, a street face, a newspaper image, and *it was suddenly so very wrong that he had begun to cry, not at death, but at the thought of not crying at death*, a silly empty man near a silly empty woman . . . (p. 40. Italics added)

His sorrow is caused, not by something wrong that has happened, but rather by what has not happened in his relationship with Mildred; the empty, impersonal nature of their relationship and the fact that two human beings could exist in such a way appalled Montag. Given such a man, who felt rather than understood what it means to be human, it is not surprising to see Montag reacting violently to the fate of the old woman who was burned with her books (p. 32ff). That incident, understandably, causes the "illness" which leads to Montag's absence from his duties. The undeniable, irrepressible sensitivity of the man thus leads to the crisis which results in his escape.

The conclusion is inevitable, for Montag is an idealist. He displays this aspect of his nature most clearly in his eventual reaction to his society. Once convinced of the error of his society, he wishes to take action, no matter what the cost. Faber, for example, is more practical and more cautious. He actually describes Montag as "a hopeless romantic" (p. 73), and the fireman virtually bullies the professor into action (p. 79). However, in spite of all Faber's whispered warnings, Montag persists in exercising his unbridled idealism. Thus he reads poetry to Mildred's friends (p. 90), an action which ultimately leads to the burning of Montag's house and to his status as a criminal and outcast. None of this, of course, is meant to imply that Montag is wrong in what he does. Without his decision to act on the strength of his convictions, the novel would lose much of its excitement and suspense. However, his naivete in assuming that he can battle the system without detection, his willingness to act immediately and spontaneously on the basis of his new ideas, his assumption that he can change the attitudes of Mrs. Bowles and Mrs. Phelps,—all betray the romantic, idealistic nature of Montag. Nowhere is that idealism, now hopefully tempered by experience, more apparent than in the words he intends to offer to his colleagues at the end of the novel, for those words are the idealistic vision of St. John:

> And on either side of the river was there a tree of life, which bare twelve manner of fruits, and yielded her fruit every month; And the leaves of the tree were for the healing of the nations. (p. 147)

Yet there are occasions on which Montag shows that his visionary romanticism is empowered by striking resourcefulness. He cannot be dismissed as an impractical dreamer. He possesses courage and ingenuity. Seemingly isolated in his society, an "outsider" forced to hide his troubled thoughts, he conceives a plan of action which enables him to communicate with others who share his point of view. Thus, he contacts Faber and suggests having books printed and he placed books in the houses of firemen in order to destroy the system they must fight. Later, his decisiveness enables him to escape, for he kills Beatty, disarms his fellow firemen and destroys the pursuing Hound. His ingenuity helps to divert suspicion from Faber, with the trick of the lawn sprinklers, and leads to the failure of the thrilling manhunt that is watched on television by all the citizens of the city. The poet in Montag does not render him ineffective as a hero. His physical courage is impressive, especially in contrast to Faber's self-confessed cowardice (p. 80), and his resourcefulness does not only lead to his successful flight, but also prompts in us the same kind of confidence in the human race which Granger expresses:

> . . . But that's the wonderful thing about man; he never gets so discouraged or disgusted that he gives up doing it all over again, because he knows very well it is important and *worth* the doing. (p. 137)

As the son and the grandson of a fireman, Montag had

scarcely had any measure of choice in deciding the course of his life. However, after ten years as a fireman—at the age of thirty—his innate sensitivity would not be denied; his buried feelings were revived, at first haltingly by the encounter with Faber in the park, later strongly and irresistibly by his relationship with Clarisse. The result is one of the most fascinating aspects of *Fahrenheit 451*: the quest of a man in search of a new self. His warm humanity, his courage and his resourcefulness lead to his personal triumph and makes Montag a fitting hero for the novel.

CLARISSE McCLELLAN

Clarisse is a high-school girl, aged seventeen, whose parents and uncle are Montag's neighbours. Though she appears in the novel only briefly, her contribution as a character is significant, because she acts as the catalyst for change in Montag. She is so different from the rest of society in her conversation, her interests and her behaviour that she not only stirs long-buried feelings in Montag, but also provides a kind of objective reality by which Montag can judge his society and measure his own spiritual condition. Thus, for example, he describes her as a mirror in which he found himself reflected (p. 10). It is Clarisse who raises the question of Montag's happiness, so that he is forced to conclude that he "wore his happiness like a mask" (p. 11). It is Clarisse who causes Montag's acute examination of his life in general and his marriage in particular. As a result, he changed irrevocably. After meeting Clarisse, he felt that the world, the world in which he had lived and which he had simply accepted, "had melted down and sprung up in a new and colorless form" (p. 15). He could never be the same again, for she had brought him to the kind of spiritual turmoil necessary for the kind of re-birth he experienced in the novel:

> One drop of rain. Clarisse. Another drop. Mildred. A third. The uncle. A fourth. The fire tonight. One, Clarisse. Two, Mildred, Three, uncle. Four, fire. One, Mildred, two, Clarisse. One, two three, four, five, Clarisse, Mildred, uncle, fire, sleeping tablets, men, disposable tissue, coattails, blow, wad, flush, Clarisse, Mildred, uncle, fire, tablets, tissues, blow, wad, flush. One two, three, one, two, three! Rain. The storm. The uncle laughing. Thunder falling downstairs. The whole world pouring down. The fire rushing up in a volcano. All rushing on down around in a spouting roar and rivering stream toward morning.
>
> (p. 16)

Such is the maelstrom of thoughts and feelings in which he is now caught that his conclusion is inevitable: "I don't know anything any more." Clarisse is the chief cause of that maelstrom.

It is easy to see why Clarisse is able to perform this role. She is completely different from the mass of people in her society. In fact, as far as society is concerned, she can be dismissed as being antisocial (p. 27). At school, she does not participate in the headlong business that others accept as normal. She objects to the frantic rushing from one organized activity to another because it does not allow for real communication between people. In her words, "Being with people is nice. But I don't think it's social to get a bunch of people together and then not let them talk . . ." (p. 27). She does not participate in the usual means of social expression which others find at the Fun Park or the Window Smasher or the Car Wrecker place. Her concept of what it means to be a social being is obviously very different from that of her society.

Thus, to Clarisse to be social means to be human. It means offering response to the real and the beautiful. Consequently, she is responsive to the feel and the smell of rain (p. 19); she is amused by the golden shininess of a dandelion rubbed under the chin (p. 20); and she is conscious of the cinnamon-like smell of old leaves (p. 26). To Clarisse, to be human is to be aware. It is that willingness to be aware which draws her to Montag and leads her to regard him as being different from the others:

> . . . You're not like the others. I've seen a few; I *know*. When I talk, you look at me. When I said something about the moon, you looked at the moon, last night. The others would never do that. The others would walk off and leave me talking. Or threaten me. No one has time any more for anyone else. You're one of the few who put up with me. That's why I think it so strange you're a fireman, it just doesn't seem right for you, somehow. (pp. 21-22)

Further, to Clarisse being social involves responsiveness to other human beings. For that reason, she obviously deplores the violence of her society. When she observes the way in which people hurt one another, she feels alienated; in her word, she feels "ancient" (p. 27). To be responsive to others involves the acceptance of responsibility for one's self and for other people, and that is the quality she finds to be lacking in her society:

> . . . I'm afraid of children my own age. They kill each other. Did it always use to be that way? My uncle says no. Six of my friends have been shot in the last year alone. Ten of them died in car wrecks. I'm afraid of them and they don't like me because I'm afraid. My uncle says his grandfather remembered when children didn't kill each other. But that was a long time ago when they had things different. They believed in responsibility, my uncle says. Do you know, I'm responsible. I was spanked when I needed it, years ago. And I do all the shopping and housecleaning by hand. (pp. 27-28)

Finally, to be a social being, in Clarisse's view, evidently means to be interested in communicating with others in a real way. It means talking with others meaningfully. Thus her home life emphasizes conversation. For example, on one occasion, Montag seems a little surprised that all the lights at her home are turned on, and he asks why that should be. Her reply is simple, direct and instructive: "Oh, just my mother and father and uncle sitting around, talking. It's like being a pedestrian, only rarer." Moreover, as we have seen, Clarisse's great objection to school is that it does not allow time for people to converse with one another. Further, her criticism of her society is that people do not talk meaningfully to one another: people, she says, do not really talk about anything:

No, not anything. They name a lot of cars or clothes or swimming pools mostly and say how swell! But they all say the same things and nobody says anything different from anybody else   (p. 28)

It is entirely fitting, therefore, that Montag finds in her face "a kind of gentle hunger that touched over everything with tireless curiosity" (p. 5). Warm and human, she is sensitive to the natural world, which she beholds with "pale surprise." She is truly human, and as such she is a suitable catalyst to revive the human feelings within Montag. Her death—the result of being run over by a car—is a grim illustration of the heedless inhumanity and irresponsibility of the society in which she lived. Her society, the event, seems to declare, is mercilessly destructive of all that is human.

MILDRED MONTAG

Mildred, the wife of Guy Montag, has known her husband ten years (p. 39). She is thirty years of age, and yet in comparison with Clarisse, who is seventeen, she seems less mature at times. The difference in age obviously masks a difference in character. That difference is evident in many aspects of the lives and personalities of the two women.

The difference is, first, obviously that between warmth and coldness. Because of her interest in people, Clarisse radiates warmth, as we have seen. Mildred, on the other hand, is constantly associated with coldness. In the darkness of the bedroom (p. 11), Montag imagines his wife "stretched on the bed, uncovered and cold, like a body displayed on the lid of a tomb." At the same time, he describes the bedroom as "the cold marbled room of a mausoleum" and the bed as "cold".

In the second place, whereas Clarisse is associated with conversation, Mildred is constantly associated with silence. Thus,

Clarisse impresses Montag with her ability to communicate on a human level. She had an "incredible power of identification" (p. 10). To Montag, "she was like the eager watcher of a marionette show, anticipating each flicker of an eyelid, each gesture of his hand, each flick of a finger, the moment before it began." In contrast, even with Mildred there, the room was truly empty. She did not inhabit a situation and fill it with a sense of her presence; she escaped from it:

> . . . Every night the waves came in and bore her off on their great tides of sound, floating her, wide-eyed, toward morning. There had been no night in the last two years that Mildred had not swum that sea, had not gladly gone down in it for the third time. (p. 11)

Typical of Mildred is her expertise at lip-reading (p. 17). So addicted is she to the little Seashells, that she wears them constantly in her ears and thus engages in laconic conversation without hearing her husband's voice.

Further, Mildred lives a second-hand life. Clarisse, of course, is illuminated by an alert curiosity about the world. Mildred, in contrast, lives in a trance-like state, "her eyes wide and staring at the fathoms of blackness above her in the ceiling" (p. 38). Her dearest wish is not to know more about the real world and real people, but to enter a substitute world of imaginary people. For that reason she wants a fourth wall-TV (p. 19); then, "it'd be just like this room wasn't ours at all, but all kinds of exotic people's rooms."

It is clear that Clarisse represents the personal element in human existence, whilst Mildred illustrates the coldly impersonal. Clarisse is interested in people; she observes them, and listens to them. Mildred never exists on this personal level. She cannot remember, for example, when she first met her husband. She has only vague interest in Clarisse. She forgets to tell Montag that Clarisse is dead (p. 43); even so, she is not sure if that is what has happened to the girl. Later (p. 45), when Montag tells her of the death of the old woman who was burned with her books, Mildred ignores what her husband has said and busies herself cleaning the rug. When Montag persists in trying to impress upon her the horror of the woman's death, Mildred replies, "She's nothing to me; she shouldn't have had books" (p. 46). The old woman's death is mere "water under the bridge." Mildred's interest is not in people; it is in things. Thus her greatest fear is that Montag will become too upset over the old woman and that consequently their material existence will be threatened: "She's got you going and the next thing you know we'll be out, no house, no job, nothing" (p. 46). Later, when disaster strikes and Montag's house is burned, her greatest concern is over the loss of her TV family: "Poor family, poor family, oh everything gone, everything, everything gone now . . ." (p. 101).

There can be no doubt that Mildred is the typical product of her society. Not caring about conversation, which can be symbolic of a human bond between people, she submerges herself in the life of her fictional family. Her greatest delight is to become part of that 'family', for only the 'family' is 'people' (p. 75). Therefore, she is in fact less than human. She is empty, a fact which Montag stresses in imagining her death:

> Montag, falling flat, going down, saw or felt, or imagined he saw or felt the walls go dark in Millie's face, heard her screaming, because in the millionth part of time left, she saw her own face reflected there, in a mirror instead of a crystal ball, and *it was such a wild, empty face*, all by itself in the room, touching nothing, starved and eating of itself, that at last she recognized it as her own and looked quickly up at the ceiling as it and the entire structure of the hotel blasted down upon her. . . (p. 142 Italics added)

Mildred is thus pathetically the novel's most vivid example of the spiritual destruction wrought by society. Existing in a trance-like unreality, she is the measure of the problems facing her world and of the challenge confronting her husband. Faced by the horror of her automaton-like existence, one can hardly conclude that the novel deals with trivial matters. That horror is only increased by the fact that in the end she betrays her husband to the authorities.

THE "OPERATORS"

These are the two men, not given names, who arrive at Montag's house to treat Mildred following her overdose of pills (p. 13ff). The fact that they are not given names emphasizes, of course, their lack of humanity.

There is no hint, in their treatment of Mildred, that they are dealing with a crisis involving a human life. Thus, "The entire operation was not unlike the digging of a trench in one's yard" (p. 13). The process is completely mechanical, with an Eye blindly searching, probing, pushing and pumping. The men contribute no sense of human feelings, even as they talk about what they are doing:

> 'Got to clean 'em out both ways,' said the operator, standing over the silent woman. 'No use getting the stomach if you don't clean the blood. Leave that stuff in the blood and the blood hits the brain like a mallet, bang, a couple thousand times and the brain just gives up, just quits.' (p. 13-14)

The men are evidently victims of their society. What they are dealing with is not an unusual case of human misery. It is a commonplace happening to them. They have to deal with nine or ten similar cases each night (p. 14). When society at large is so indifferent to the condition of human beings, then individuals can hardly be expected to be any more compassionate in their actions and attitudes. Casual and impersonal, the operators are a striking illustration of human emptiness in *Fahrenheit 451*.

CAPTAIN BEATTY

Captain Beatty, Montag's superior officer at the fire-station, is one of the few fully-developed characters in the novel. Apart from Montag himself, the others appear either very briefly or else have only one aspect of personality which is stressed. For example, while Mildred plays an important role in the novel, it is only her death-in-life condition which is emphasized to any great extent. However, with Beatty the situation is different. There are many aspects to his personality. He is not merely a dedicated, mindless automaton. He impresses the reader with the depth of his character: he is observant, watchful, shrewd, intelligent, educated and ruthless. As such, he provides a remarkable adversary for the hero.

Beatty's shrewd watchfulness is evident early in the novel. When we first meet him, Montag has been upset by the belligerent reaction of the Hound (p. 22ff). Guy's nervousness does not escape attention, and as Beatty stands looking at him, there is the suggestion of more than casual interest in his apparently idle question, "You got a guilty conscience about something?" As he shows later, Beatty is quick to perceive the first signs of distress in his men. He notices that Montag continues to be nervous of the Hound and mentions the fireman's entering the station by the back door (p. 29); he observes Montag's preoccupied mood (p. 30). No doubt Montag's question as to whether firemen had at one time been called to put out fires (p. 31-32) confirms Beatty's growing suspicions. Thus, when Montag is so distressed over the burning of the old woman with her books, Beatty is not deceived by the pretended sickness, and he makes a point of calling upon Montag. The Captain has diagnosed the real situation. He knows the problem, without Montag's having to say anything. As he observes, "Every fireman, sooner or later, hits this" (p. 49). It is clear that little escapes Beatty's attention. He knows of Montag's meetings with Clarisse; he seems to know that Montag possesses a book, even before the fireman gives any clue to that fact (p. 57); and while Montag is struggling with his seemingly-secret anxieties, Beatty sends the Hound to the fireman's home (p. 100).

This shrewdness is entirely congruent with the Captain's education and intelligence. He is not a mindless servant of his society. He understands its purposes and its dynamics. Thus, his explanation of the evolution of his society is lucid, precise and comprehensive. He is able to explain to Montag (pp. 49-56), not only what happened in the past to produce their society, but also the significance of those events. He understands very well what has happened to the level of culture; he sees it clearly for what it is—"a sort of paste pudding norm" (p. 50). However, his satisfaction with the present state of things (p. 56) is not based upon ignorance. He is well-versed in the literature of the past. One of the most tense scenes in the novel is that in which Beatty baits Montag by confusing the fireman with contradictory quotations from literature (p. 94ff). His method for browbeating Montag is as clever as it is cynical:

> 'Oh, you were scared silly,' said Beatty, for I was doing a terrible thing in using the very books you clung to, to rebut you on every hand, on every point! What traitors books can be! you think they're backing you up, and they turn on you. Others can use them, too, and there you are, lost in the middle of the moor, in a great welter of nouns and verbs and adjectives. (p. 97)

In the midst of this struggle, Faber describes Beatty as "slippery" (p. 96). The description is unworthy of the Captain. Beatty is much more than devious and cunning. He is clever, and he is well prepared to combat the heresy he seeks to destroy. Montag, of course, wins the final battle, in that Montag lives and Beatty dies. But that final battle is physical in nature. In all other ways except one—namely, that he fails to convince Montag of his error—Beatty triumphs, for he confuses the fireman, exposes him for what he is and destroys his place in society.

Such a character is well-fitted to play an important role in the plot of the novel, and Beatty's contribution should not be underestimated. He is the means by which Montag's inner tension is brought into sharp focus. His shrewd observation of the fireman's growing tension objectifies Montag's anxieties. Thus the Captain's role contributes to the suspense of many scenes. He is also the instrument by which Bradbury communicates to us the history of the horrifying society in the novel. Further, Beatty sets in motion the events which lead to Montag's becoming a fugitive. In all of these aspects, Beatty symbolizes, then, not only the sheer physical power of the society he serves, but also the intelligent, informed nature of that power. In this, he is a worthy adversary for the hero.

And, remarkably, Beatty is complex to the end. In the moment of final confrontation with Montag, the Captain had seemingly invited death: "*Beatty wanted to die*" (p. 108). One can only conclude that there must have been a weak point in Beatty's cynicism. The master whose mind could roam vast territories in literature perhaps could not really resist what he had read. The shrewd intelligence had perhaps taken to heart the futility of its master's task in society. Beatty's reasons for wanting to die are not explained and speculations about them are as tormenting as they are enigmatic. However, given a man of such ability, shrewdness and intelligence, it hardly seems likely that he could have avoided being convinced, however unwillingly and however vaguely, by the very literature he claimed to despise.

That his death should have ironic overtones is most fitting. Beatty died by fire, the very fire he regarded as a source of cleansing. Equally ironically, he was the man who wore on his hat the sign of the Phoenix, that mythical bird which was reputed to be consumed by fire every five hundred years, only to rise to new life from the ashes. Thus, in keeping with the complexity of the man, Beatty had displayed what was apparently a symbol of destruction, but what in actual fact is really a symbol of regeneration.

STONEMAN AND BLACK

Stoneman and Black are the two firemen who are fellow crewmembers of Montag at the fire-station. They appear infrequently in the novel and are usually associated with one another. Thus they are never really given separate identities. Like Rosencrantz and Guildenstern in *Hamlet*, they are not individuals; their association with one another and with their work is their identity. Consequently, in their lack of individuality they come to represent typical firemen in the society of the novel.

Stoneman is involved in one incident which might be regarded as unusual. He is driving the fire-truck on the return to the station from the house of the old woman who was burned with her books (p. 37). For some reason, he misses the turn which leads to the station. The explanation for his lapse appears to be his surprise at Beatty's quoting the words of Latimer, which the old woman had echoed. It may be that he is surprised to hear his captain uttering such words. That interpretation, however, would imply that such an action by Beatty was unusual, and that is hardly plausible in the light of Beatty's mastery of literary allusion elsewhere in the novel. The captain quotes from literature with such ease and familiarity later in the book that its use as a technique can hardly have been so new. There is a second possibility, which can be understood by setting Stoneman's surprise in context. None of the firemen was unaffected by the old woman's death. On the way back to the firehouse they neither looked at one another nor spoke; they simply stared straight ahead, silently. Thus, when Stoneman heard the words of Latimer perhaps the fireman was stirred even more by the evening's work. Forgotten emotional chords perhaps stirred responsively. However, the moment should not be unduly emphasized. There is no other indication in the book that Stoneman has any thoughts which might be considered even vaguely seditious. The more typical role of Stoneman and Black is illustrated later, for they are on duty when the firemen raid Montag's house. When Montag kills Beatty horrifyingly (p. 105-106), they do nothing, and Montag easily renders them powerless by knocking them unconscious.

The only occasion on which Black is mentioned separately occurs when Montag hides books in Black's house (p. 115). This is the only example of Montag's acting on the plan that Faber and he had conceived earlier to discredit firemen by hiding books in their homes. The incident hardly creates any feelings of sympathy for Black; one could not feel human sympathy for a character who never emerges as a human being.

The two firemen, then, do not play a dynamic role in the novel. They are more part of the social setting than part of the characterization. Their names are, in fact, all that they are and probably indicate all that we need to know about them. 'Stoneman' suggests someone without feeling; 'Black' has connotations of darkness and therefore, in terms of the theme of the book, suggests someone without illumination in a metaphorical sense.

THE OLD WOMAN

The old woman burned with her books (pp. 32-36) is not identified by name. She is simply a woman possessing books who has been betrayed by her neighbour, a Mrs. Blake. However, the old woman's behaviour takes on heroic proportions. Though the firemen reduce her house to a shambles as they throw her books in a heap and though she is slapped by Beatty, she is resolute and determined. Fully aware of the significance of what is happening, she is the person used to introduce Latimer's challenging words into the novel. Moreover, she is defiant to the end. Not only does she die with her books; she even lights the match which ignites the kerosene.

Thus, though her appearance is brief, the effect she has is profound and far-reaching. The firemen themselves are not unaffected by the manner of her death. On the way back to the firehouse, they are silent. Only Beatty seems able to dismiss her death as the foolish act of a fanatic. For Montag, the moment is climactic. The woman creates a feeling which he is unable to ignore. The recollection of her death torments Montag and seems to bring into sharper focus his dissatisfaction and his doubt. He cannot, like Mildred (p. 46), simply dismiss the woman as being of no importance. The memory of a woman who could choose to die so horribly for her books commits him to asking the questions and seeking the answers which finally lead to his rebellion.

Obviously, then, the old woman, though not a major character, plays a major role in the plot. Her experience provides the important incident which helps Montag, on the one hand, to clarify the significance of his encounters with Clarisse, and, on the other hand, to see more clearly the nature of Mildred's predicament. Finally, of course, the old woman also illustrates the nature of the opposition to the dominant society in the novel. Through her, we see that all is not well in the state and receive assurance that noble, human ideals are not dead. Men and women may die for their faith, but the noble flame is not extinguished:

> Be of good comfort, Master Ridley, and play the man. We shall this day light such a candle, by God's grace, in England, as I trust shall never be put out.

PROFESSOR FABER

Professor Faber is "a retired English Professor who had been thrown out upon the world forty years ago when the last liberal arts college shut for lack of students and patronage" (p. 66). Thus he is one of the obviously large company of academics that the social system had, in one way or another, forced into exile. For example, Granger introduces Montag (p. 133) to a number of such academics—Professor Clement, Dr. Simmons, Professor West and Reverend Padover. Granger himself had written several books.

Our first encounter with Faber gives the impression that he is the stereotype of the academic. He is old, and looks as though he has not left his house in years. His apparent frailty is confirmed by the paleness of his appearance:

> . . . He and the white plaster walls inside were much the same. There was white in the flesh of his mouth and his cheeks and his hair was white and his eyes had faded, with white in the vague blueness
> there.   (p. 71-72)

Moreover, he lacks physical courage, which is not a virtue typical of the stereotype he represents. When Montag arrives at Faber's house, the professor is "very much afraid." He is quite frank in describing his cowardice:

> . . . Mr. Montag, you are looking at a coward. I saw the way things were going, a long time back. I said nothing. I'm one of the innocents who could have spoken up and out when no one would listen to the 'guilty,' but I did not speak and thus became guilty myself. And when finally they set the structure to burn the books, using the firemen, I grunted a few times and subsided, for there were no others grunting and yelling with me, by then. Now, it's too late. (p. 73)

However, the character of Professor Faber is not entirely negative. He has that knowledge and insight Montag needs to begin his quest in earnest. For example (p. 73f), he helps Montag to understand much more clearly just what he is searching for. All the fireman seems to sense is that "something's missing" in his life, and that perhaps the something can be found in books. Faber informs the fireman that it is not just books he needs; Montag needs what it was that the books contained. The books, he declares, are valuable because "they stitched the patches of the universe together into one garment for us" (p. 74). Further, Faber proceeds to explain in some detail what he means by that statement. Thus we learn that, in Faber's view, three things are necessary in the present situation: quality of information, which books can provide; leisure to digest the information; and the right to carry out actions based on what we learn from the interaction of the first two. This kind of analysis shows very clearly the importance of Faber's role as a tutor to Montag.

However, the value of Faber's knowledge and insight does not end there. Faber plays an important part in the structure of the novel. This can be realized when the professor is seen as a force counterbalancing the presence of Captain Beatty. Like Beatty, Faber is an important influence in Montag's life. Also like Beatty, Faber offers, at a crucial stage of the novel, a detailed analysis of present society. Both men have the shrewdness and the knowledge to undertake this task. Their points of view are, of course, quite different, in that they are on different sides in the conflict. But both represent intellectual forces which are to be reckoned with. Their roles are probably seen most clearly in the scene at the firehouse, when Beatty torments Montag with conflicting quotations from literature. For at that time Montag is the audience for two voices, one the insistent whispering of Faber, the other the insistent contemptuousness of Beatty. However, the two long speeches, one by Beatty (p. 49ff) and one by Faber (p. 73ff), should not be disregarded in a study of the novel. These speeches emphasize the role which Faber on the one hand and Beatty on the other plays in the development of the book.

In addition, it must be remembered that it is Faber's knowledge which enables him to communicate with Montag. Fearful though he was, Faber had sacrificed a great deal in order to obtain the electronic equipment needed to build the tiny transmitter by which he communicated with the fireman. Further, Faber has the knowledge necessary to turn Montag's desires in a practical direction. Because he knows an unemployed printer, he conceives the plan whereby they might be able to have more books printed (p. 79). In this way, the printer serves to point to signs of hope in the desperate situation; he gives assurance of the persistence and quality of the opposition and survives to provide expectations of renaissance (p. 141).

Faber's contribution to the novel is of great importance. In terms of simple contribution to plot development, he provides Montag with the essential contact with a vanishing way of life and provides the fireman with the impetus needed to continue his quest. In terms of contribution to structure, Faber is the force which parallels the opposing force represented by Beatty. In terms of the contribution to the hero's dilemma, Faber is, for a while, Montag's *alter ego*, that aspect of the fireman which is struggling to emerge. This last contribution is one which Montag acknowledges openly:

> . . . In the days to follow, and in the nights when there was no moon and in the nights when there was a very bright moon shining on the earth, the old man would go on with this talking and this talking, drop by drop, stone by stone, flake by flake. His mind would well over at last and he would not be Montag any more, this the old man told him, assured him, promised him. He would be Montag-plus-Faber, fire plus water, and then, one day, after everything had mixed and simmered and worked away in silence, there would be neither fire nor water, but wine. *Out of two separate and opposite things, a third.* (p. 92-93 Italics added)

MRS. ANN BOWLES AND MRS. CLARA PHELPS

These two women are considered together because they are together on the only occasion upon which we meet them in the novel and because their characters are so alike that it is difficult to consider them as individuals.

Both of the women are central figures in the dramatic scene in which they visit Mildred in order to watch television (p. 83ff). They show themselves to be not only remarkably like one another, but also remarkably like Mildred. All of the women engage in the same kind of inane conversation:

'Doesn't everyone look nice!'
'Nice.'
'You look fine, Millie!'
'Fine.'
'Everyone looks swell.'
'Swell!'

During the television show, which features bodies flying through the air following crashes involving jet cars, the women reveal complete indifference to human suffering. One merely exclaims, "Millie, did you *see* that!" Millie's reply is: "I saw it, I *saw* it!" Mrs. Phelps displays the same indifference, even toward her husband. Their husbands, she explains, come and go, according to the demands of the army. Her husband, Pete, will not be back until next week, but she is not worried. She lets "old Pete" do the worrying. In any case, Pete and she have an understanding about their relationship:

> . . . Pete and I always said, no tears, nothing like that. It's our third marriage each and we're independent. Be independent, we always said. He said, if I get killed off, you just go right ahead and don't cry, but get married again, and don't think of me. (p. 85)

It is ironic—and typical of the world of *Fahrenheit 451*—that this bleak picture of marriage reminds Mildred of a five-minute romance she saw on television the previous night! In real life or on television, perhaps five minutes is all that the empty people of the novel could endure in a relationship! Montag's reaction to their inane conversation provides a telling description of their true nature:

> Montag said nothing but stood looking at the women's faces as he had once looked at the faces of saints in a strange church he had entered when he was a child. The faces of those enameled creatures meant nothing to him, though he talked to them and stood in that church for a long time, trying to be of that religion, trying to know what that religion was, trying to get enough of the raw incense and special dust of the place into his lungs and thus into his blood to feel touched and concerned by the meaning of the colorful men and women with the porcelain eyes and the blood-ruby lips. But there was nothing, nothing; it was a stroll through another store, and his currency strange and unusable there, and his passion cold, even when he touched the wood and plaster and clay. So it was now, in his own parlor, with these women twisting in their chairs under his gaze, lighting cigarettes, blowing smoke, touching their sun-fired hair and examining their blazing fingernails as if they had caught fire from his look. (p. 85-86)

It need occasion no surprise, then, to notice that these vapid women, incapable of a warm relationship in marriage, have no love for children. Mrs. Phelps states emphatically that she does not want any children, for "No one in his right mind, the Good Lord knows, would have children!" Mrs. Bowles has had two children, but both, on her insistence, had been delivered by Caesarian section, because there was "No use going through all that agony for a baby." Further, her attitude toward her children is entirely in keeping with her character and with the nature of her society:

'I plunk the children in school nine days out of ten. I put up with them when they come home three days a month; it's not bad at all. You heave them into the parlor and turn the switch. It's like washing clothes; stuff laundry in and slam the lid.' Mrs. Bowles tittered. 'They'd just as soon kick as kiss me. Thank God, I can kick back!'
(p. 86-87)

The women fare no better in their vain attempt to discuss politics. They all, it seems, voted for President Noble in the last election because, in Mrs. Bowles' words, "he's one of the nicest looking men ever became president." They express indignation about the man who opposed the president in the election. To begin with, his name— Hubert Hoag—could hardly be compared with that of Winston Noble. Further, Mr. Hoag was a short, fat man, in contrast to Mr. Noble, who was tall. In view of this superficiality, it is fitting that the women are distressed when Montag shows them a volume of poetry. Mrs. Bowles declares flatly that she hates poetry and wants to go home. Their distress is not alleviated when Montag reads to them. Mrs. Phelps weeps, and Mrs. Bowles is very angry that their host should have read the "silly awful hurting words." On some level at least, the poetry had obviously been communicated to them. But the communication is neither long-lasting nor truly meaningful. Mrs. Bowles and Mrs. Phelps report Montag's conduct to the firemen, and as a result his house is destroyed and he becomes a fugitive. The women are obviously devoid of human feeling. They are hollow at the core, having no true existence of their own. They are exact duplicates of T. S. Eliot's "hollow men", in the poem with that title, who are merely straw-filled scarecrows, whispering together with the sound of the wind over dry grass. Their experience is summed up in another of Eliot's poems, from *The Four Quartets*:

>   The strained time-ridden faces
> Distracted from distraction by distraction
> Filled with fancies and empty of meaning
> Tumid apathy with no concentration
> Men and bits of paper, whirled by the cold wind
> That blows before and after time . . .
> Internal darkness, deprivation
> And destitution of all property,
> Desiccation of the world of sense,
> Evacuation of the world of fancy,
> Inoperancy of the world of spirit . . .   (*Burnt Norton*, III)

Being such vacant creatures, Mrs. Bowles and Mrs. Phelps obviously serve as vivid and discomforting reminders of the cultural and intellectual emptiness of their society. They are typical less-than-human inhabitants of a less-than-human world. Yet they contribute to the positive evil of that society by their betrayal of Montag. Their action confirms their emptiness.

In addition, Mrs. Bowles and Mrs. Phelps play a minor role in the structure of the novel. They are the female counterparts of Stoneman and Black. True, more elaboration of the characters of the women is offered than is the case with the men. However, lengthy elaboration is not required with the latter. We can understand the condition of the firemen from the actions in which they take part; their silent acquiescence is indication enough of what they are like. The elaboration of the women, though, confirms the impression of domestic life that we have received from the marriage of the Montags. Thus, the pairing of the two women, Mrs. Bowles and Mrs. Phelps, with the two firemen, Stoneman and Black, appears to be one of many such pairings in the novel. For example, there are two women—Mildred and Clarisse—who are close to Montag and who offer sharp contrasts in personality. Beatty and Faber are another such pair, one being the voice of society and the other the voice of culture and humanity. Further, Montag—as Montag the fireman—and Faber are paired in the kind of relationship seen in that between the *ego* and the *alter-ego*. These links between characters can scarcely be dismissed as being either inconsequential or accidental. In a minor way, then, Mrs. Bowles and Mrs. Phelps contribute to that "twinning" technique in the structure by virtue of the fact that they are the female counterparts of Stoneman and Black.

GRANGER

Granger is one of the leaders of the exiles who have been driven from the cities by the activities of the firemen. He is an author who appears to have a special interest in sociology and philosophy. He has written a book called *The Fingers in the Glove; the Proper Relationship between the Individual and Society.* The title might be regarded as giving some clue to Granger's thought, in that it seems to imply that the individual should bear the same relationship to society as fingers to a glove. That is, the fingers in a glove are a part—and a harmonious, integral part—of the concept of glove, while retaining their identity as fingers, being separate and distinct in terms of size and location. So, it might be said, with the individual in society. He should be part of the total, unified concept known as society, but nonetheless be separate and distinct in terms of individual qualities and functions. Granger's philosophical bent is confirmed by the fact that he *is* Plato's *Republic*; he is the exile who has committed to memory that particular work of the Greek philosopher.

Granger is an exile because he, too, came into conflict with his society. Years ago he struck a fireman who came to his house to burn his library (p. 134). It is fitting, therefore, that Granger should confirm the kind of outlook expressed earlier in the novel by Faber. In recalling his memories of his grandfather, Granger offers confirmation of what Faber had tried to make Montag understand: that books in themselves are not important and that it is what books represent and preserve that is important. Therefore, for example, Granger explains that when his grandfather died he had not wept for the old man, but for what the old man had been in his life and for what would no longer be experienced in view of his death:

> . . . And when he died, I suddenly realized that I wasn't crying for him at all, but for all the things he did. I cried because he would never do them again, he would never carve another piece of wood or help us raise doves and pigeons in the back yard or play the violin the way he did. He was part of us and when he died, all the actions stopped dead and there was no one to do them just the way he did. He was individual. He was an important man. I've never gotten over his death. Often I think, what wonderful carvings never came to birth because he died. How many jokes are missing from the world, and how many homing pigeons untouched by his hands. He shaped the world. He *did* things to the world. He shaped the world. He *did* things to the world. The world was bankrupted of ten million fine actions the night he passed on. (p. 139)

Granger thus emphasizes an important aspect of the theme of the novel with his re-affirmation of the importance of the individual, not for his social function, but for what he is.

Granger also serves to clarify the *dénouement* of the novel. He expresses the technique by which society will be changed. There is, we see through Granger, a technique for survival. Through him we learn—if we wish to express the concept in metaphorical terms—that though Israel might be destroyed, a saving remnant will remain to establish a new Israel. The books, he reveals, have become the men. The future is safe *in* the people. Out of this concept emerges Montag's new role. The former fireman will be their *Book of Ecclesiastes*. When the rest of the world destroys itself, as it surely will, he will, with the others, appear to offer the knowledge that they think will be needed.

Thus, through Granger we see that Montag has arrived at his spiritual destination. That realization is complete with a final, ironic thrust from Granger, when he reveals that they, too, are book-burners. They destroyed books only that they might preserve in more permanent form—in the memories of men—what was in the books. In this way, Montag the book-burner has become, again, Montag the book-burner. But it is a new Montag and a new reason for destruction. The irony, with its grim humour, serves to emphasize the distinction.

Granger is the last major portrait in the novel, and he obviously possesses qualities which make him an ideal leader among the exiles. He is clearly both an intellectual and an idealist: he has written a book, and expresses strong faith in the capacity of man to prevail:

> . . . And when the war's over, some day, some year, the books can be written again, the people will be called in, one by one, to recite what they know and we'll set it up in type until another Dark Age, when we might have to do the whole damn thing over again. But that's the wonderful thing about man; he never gets so discouraged or disgusted that he gives up doing it all over again, because he knows very well it is important and *worth* the doing. (p. 137)

And yet he is both shrewd and practical. For example, as they watch the police pursuit of Montag on television, Granger forecasts the outcome—that the police will find a scapegoat, an innocent victim who is said to be Montag. Moreover, Granger has survived in exile for a number of years and is obviously party to the group's plans for the future. It is not surprising, therefore, that Granger serves two important functions in the novel: to clarify the theme and to indicate to the reader what the future will be.

OTHER CHARACTERS

A number of other people are mentioned by name in the novel. However, they do not play an important role in the action and, except for their names, we are given little information about them. They are, therefore, simply listed below.

Fred Clement, one of the exiles, is a "former occupant of the Thomas Hardy chair at Cambridge in the years before it became an Atomic Engineering School" (p. 133).

Dr. Simmons, another exile, is a former professor from the University College of Los Angeles, where he taught Spanish literature, since he is a specialist in Ortega y Gasset.

Professor West, also an exile, taught ethics at Columbia University.

Reverend Padover, another of the exiles, is a minister who "lost his flock between one Sunday and the next for his views" (p. 134).

Harris (p. 134) lives in Youngstown and has memorized the Book of Ecclessiastes.

Mr. Simmons (p. 135) has memorized the work of Marcus Aurelius.

SETTING

The setting of *Fahrenheit 451* is at once distinctive and deceptive. It is distinctive in that Bradbury has created for his characters a world that has remarkable and unique features which are totally foreign and strange to our way of life. If we were called upon to walk the streets of the unusual city created by Bradbury, we would, for example, immediately have brought to our attention the lack of idle conversations as pedestrians passed by and the speed at which the traffic drove in the streets. Yet the setting is also deceptive in its recognizable features which so closely resemble those of our own world: the streets, the appearance of the people, the structures of society, the ways of everyday living are recognizable enough. The two aspects of the setting are plain enough. The reason for that is not difficult to understand. It is part of the usual technique of the writer of fantasy to create a world of the future possessing unusual features but, nonetheless, retaining sufficient recognizable features that enable the reader to recognize *his* society at the core of that future society. The comparison between the two is the source of the writer's statement.

The world of *Fahrenheit 451* is undoubtedly unusual, as a discussion of various features reveals.

Relationships have undergone change. The porches on which people used to sit chatting away their leisure hours have vanished. Any talk that there is is talk of things:

> . . . They name a lot of cars or clothes or swimming pools mostly and say how swell! But they all say the same things and nobody says anything different from anyone else. And most of the time in the cafes they have the joke-boxes on and the same jokes most of the time, or the musical wall lit and all the colored patterns running up and down, but it's only color and all abstract. (p. 28)

Relationships have deteriorated to such a degree that the relationship of marriage is devoid of affection and warmth. For example, Mildred and Guy can no longer even remember when and where they met, and Mrs. Phelps and her husband have, within marriage, established a kind of 'independence', which seems largely to mean that they are not to show deep feeling for one another. True human relationship seems to have vanished, in addition, because the people cannot trust one another. They betray one another to the authorities, a betrayal which brings the Salamander screaming to the door and results in the destruction of property and life.

True relationship has disappeared because society cherishes the principle of *self-gratification*. Mrs. Bowles, for example, detests poetry, calling it "nasty", because it brings "crying and awful feelings." Society avoids discomforting experiences and emphasizes the virtue of pleasure:

> . . . What do we want in this country, above all? People want to be happy, isn' that right? Haven't you heard it all your life? I want to be happy, people say. Well, aren't they? Don't we keep them moving, don't we give them fun? That's all we live for, isn' it? For pleasure, for titillation? (p. 54)

That is why whenever Mildred feels distressed, whenever she feels upset because of anything that Montag has said, she turns immediately to her pills. The pills enable her to escape from feelings that she cannot handle otherwise. For that very reason, society offers its men and women all manner of means to escape from emotions that they cannot manage. There are fun parks, car-wrecking-places, window-smashing establishments, joke boxes, musical walls and—not to be omitted—television walls. The latter present *ersatz* emotion, trivial situations with no real conflict. Sentimentality replaces true sentiment; passivity replaces conflict; escape takes the place of confrontation.

The world of the novel is *a world of conformity*. The emphasis is upon social integration. Clarisse is branded as anti-social because she wishes to express her individuality. Being social, to her, means conversing. To society, however, being social means engaging in organized activities that reflect solidarity with one's fellows. To be social means to be moving constantly; it means never taking time out to think. Individual reflection emphasizes, of course, individual differences. The society of the novel is directed towards sameness and not difference. That is why the opposition party is labelled as the "Outs". They have no hope of gaining power; they are an absurd alternative for the people, because society's values favour the 'in-group'. Moreover, when Montag is finally betrayed, one of the betrayers is his wife. At that time she has no feeling for Montag to influence her. Her response is inevitable. It is, in society's terms, the necessary response of the woman who is truly social.

However, it is also apparent that the world of *Fahrenheit 451* is *an unhappy world*. Suicides are common phenomena. Mildred, for example, can insist that no one can get himself killed in war, but she accepts suicide as a common form of death:

> . . . I've never known any dead man killed in a war. Killed jumping off buildings, yes, like Gloria's husband last week, but from wars? No.
>
> (p. 85)

Meaningless death is common, for the unhappiness of the people expresses itself in thoughtless violence:

> . . . I'm afraid of children my own age. They kill each other. Did it always use to be that way? My uncle says no. Six of my friends have been shot in the last year alone. Ten of them died in car wrecks. (p. 27-28)

In addition, we note the attitude of the "operators" who arrive to treat Mildred after her overdose of pills. They are not moved, as a crisis should surely move them. They are accustomed to what has happened. It is a common phenomenon. They "get these cases nine or ten a night"; there are so many cases that they have had to have special machines built! The people of the novel are not really devoid of all feeling. They have sufficient feeling left to be distressed on occasion, like Mildred and Mrs. Phelps and Mrs. Bowles. Further, the way in which Beatty appears to invite death at the hands of Montag indicates feelings that have reached the point of despair or relief. However, the dominant impression is that disturbing feelings must be shunned or banished. The unhappiness is no more than an undercurrent.

Further, the world of the novel is a world of *control by technology*. The technology is applied particularly through the medium of television. The population is absorbed in the world of transient things—the flickering, moving images on the screen, the pseudo-dramas involving the 'family', the quickly-digested information. The emphasis is upon what is instantly communicated, with no "slippery stuff like philosophy or sociology to tie things up with." The people, in that situation, do not need to be oppressed. The responses required are so minimal that after a time no deeper responses are available. Reduce culture to "a sort of paste pudding norm" and in time there is no real culture. With the disappearance of culture comes the disappearance of values. With the disappearance of values, there is a disappearance of real significance. All that is left is the *now*. Since the *now* is all-important, the inevitable conclusion is that it may as well be passed as pleasurably as possible. Thus the control sought does not need any very sophisticated technology or gadgetry for its exercise. There is no need, for example, for the sophisticated science of Huxley's *Brave New World*. The technology necessary is actually that available today and presently employed by the mass media!

When George Orwell wrote his startling novel, *Nineteen Eighty-Four*, he was not really writing about the world of the future. He was writing about his world, the society of 1948. He was writing about that world of the postwar "Cold War" in which whole populations were propagandized and in which human values were being sacrificed to political exigencies. The setting of *Fahrenheit 451* shows Ray Bradbury employing a similar technique. Some features of the setting are startling. We are beguiled by televisions employing entire living-room walls, by doors opened by means of 'glove-boxes', by thimble radios worn in the ear, by toasters that automatically butter the finished product. Most of all, we may be misled by the arresting device of using firemen to start fires instead of extinguishing them. But the really startling feature of the setting in the novel is that which needs little technology to achieve. That feature is Bradbury's portrait of a world without books. *Thus the dominant characteristic of the world of the novel is its emptiness.* That emptiness is apparent in the absence of truly human relationships, in the inability of the people to see beyond the present moment and its demands for self-gratification, in the surrender of the uniqueness of individuality, and in the lack of deep human feelings. The world is empty because the people have lost what it was that made them people. They have lost, not so much books, as what was in books. Faber saw the problem and its effects clearly:

> . . . Do you know the legend of Hercules and Antaeus, the giant wrestler, whose strength was incredible so long as he stood firmly on the earth. But when he was held, rootless, in midair, by Hercules, he perished easily. If there isn't something in that legend for us today, in this city, in our time, then I am completely insane.   (p. 74)

The entire problem, of course, is symbolized in the person of Antaeus. The people of *Fahrenheit 451* are similarly "rootless". They have lost their footing on the earth because they no longer are in communication with what is real. They have lost the books which tell of the substance of life, which could speak of the significance of human existence. They have exchanged meaning for triviality, and in the exchange have lost themselves. That is why the world of the novel is the world of the hollow people.

62

STRUCTURE

To say that structure is important in the writing of a novel should hardly need justification. Indeed, to underestimate the importance of that element in a novel is to labour under a misconception of the nature of the novel. For the novelist does not present life—the raw process in which we are involved and which we express every day— but an edited version of life, by which he seeks to communicate to us his vision and his perspective. Structure, then, is a reflection of the novelist's skill in combining the various elements of his work in such a way as to produce a sense of completeness and a feeling of aesthetic satisfaction. Virginia Woolf has expressed the matter succinctly:

> If there is one gift more essential to the novelist than another it is the power of combination—the single vision. The success of the masterpieces seems to lie not so much in their freedom from faults— indeed we tolerate the grossest errors in them all—but in the immense persuasiveness of a mind which has completely mastered its perspective.
> (Quoted by Elizabeth Drew in *The Novel: A Guide to Fifteen English Masterpieces*, p. 16)

Consequently, in any worthwhile novel we should expect to find the structure acting as a unifying element in combining and relating other elements, such as characterization and theme.

The most obvious structural device in *Fahrenheit 451* is its division into three parts: "The Hearth and the Salamander", "The Sieve and the Sand", and "Burning Bright". The need for the tripartite organization becomes apparent on considering the events included within each division.

In "The Hearth and the Salamander" section, the following are the main events:

- Montag's encounters with Clarisse
- Mildred's near-death
- Mildred's character
- the death of the old woman who was burned with her books
- Montag's exploration of his relationship with Mildred
- Montag's "illness" and Beatty's visit
- Montag begins to read

In the second section, "The Sieve and the Sand," the following significant events are presented:

- Montag's decision to communicate with Faber
- the subway ride to Faber's

- Montag's meeting with Faber
- the visit of Mildred's friends and Montag's poetry reading
- Beatty's relentless attack upon Montag at the firehouse
- the Salamander stops at Montag's house

In "Burning Bright", we witness:

- the burning of Montag's house and the death of Beatty
- the pursuit of Montag
- Montag's escape
- the revelation of the life and philosophy of the exiles
- the destruction of the city and the beginning of the future.

When the events are seen starkly in this way, the justification for the three-fold division becomes clearer. The divisions signal and unify the plot development of the novel, both on the narrative level (the "story") and also on the psychological level, which reveals the development of Montag's thinking. Thus, "The Hearth and the Salamander" brings into focus the central conflict of the novel, that between the life of the people and the activities of the firemen. The hearth is symbolic of domestic life, of the warm, cosy fire which is not destructive and which was common when people sat around and talked in their homes. The Salamander is the name by which the fire-engine is known. The salamander is, of course, a newt-like amphibian who, so legend has it, is unharmed by fire. Obviously, then, in giving this section of the book the title "The Hearth and the Salamander", Bradbury is neatly summarising the actual conflict. Consequently, in the first section Montag is pulled between the opposing forces of the hearth and the salamander.

In the second section, Montag has understood the conflict much more clearly than he had earlier, and the events show him acting on the results of his insights. This section, then, is principally one of unresolved tension. The title for the section is a clear indication of that fact. "The Sieve and the Sand" refers directly back to a childhood recollection that Montag recounts:

> Once as a child he had sat upon a yellow dune by the sea in the middle of the blue and hot summer day, trying to fill a sieve with sand, because some cruel cousin had said, 'Fill this sieve and you'll get a dime!' And the faster he poured, the faster it sifted through with a hot whispering. His hands were tired, the sand was boiling, the sieve was empty. Seated there in the midst of July, without a sound, he felt the tears move down his cheeks. (p. 69)

Montag's feelings as an adult echo those he experienced as a child, when faced by a task which was obviously too great for him and which equally obviously was the result of someone else's cruel in-

64

difference to his feelings. So, too, in Part Two of the novel, Montag is overcome by frustration. It seems to him that the task of imbibing knowledge is like the frustrating task of filling a sieve with sand. Hence the events in that section all reflect the fireman's agonizing frustration.

The title of the third section is more complex. Taken at face value, "Burning Bright" may simply refer—with ironic reference to the fire image, of course—of the faith in man which shines still in the world, and particularly in the world of the exiles. It is something that cannot be extinguished. Therefore, it might be said, "Burning Bright" provides a fitting title for that section of the novel which leads to Montag's joining the outlaws and to that beginning of the future with which the final pages deal. However, there may also be here an obscure reference to William Blake's poem, *The Tiger*:

> Tiger! Tiger! burning bright
> In the forests of the night,
> What immortal hand or eye
> Could frame thy fearful symmetry?

Blake uses the tiger to illustrate the mystery of God's creation, for the tiger is both beautiful in its power and awesome in its ferociousness. In a similar way, the situation in *Fahrenheit 451* illustrates the paradox that is man. On the one hand, man is capable of ferocious acts; on the other hand, as we see in the novel's exiles, he is capable of the most profound and compassionate faith. In the "forests of the night"—that is, where the truth will be known (among the exiles)—the resolution of the conflict will be made known. If, then, the title of the section is indeed an allusion to Blake's poem, the aptness of the reference is obvious.

Hence, it is evident that the major divisions of the novel's structure are closely connected with the novel's theme. The divisions reflect the stages of Montag's quest, not only on the purely narrative level, but also on the psychological level.

Another major feature of the structure is connected with the psychological level. That feature is the absence of division into chapters. Chapters may serve a definite function. One such function is, of course, on occasion to allow the reader to pause in his reading. The case for this function need not perhaps be expressed with the irony of Fielding in *Joseph Andrews*:

> But in reality the case is otherwise, and in this, as well as all other instances, we consult the advantage of our reader, not our own; and indeed, many notable uses arise to him from this method: for, first, those little spaces between our chapters may be looked upon as an inn

> or resting-place, where he may stop and take a glass, or any other refreshment, as it pleases him. (Book II, Chapter 1)

Nonetheless, chapter divisions can be seen to serve a purpose, depending on the nature of the novel. In *Fahrenheit 451*, the absence of chapter divisions is purposeful. After all, an important aspect of the novel is the communication of Montag's inner state. He has to be shown to be a man under stress, a man suffering from inner and not only outer conflict. Thus, the absence of chapter headings gives the narrative that sense of fluidity needed to convey a state of mind. Events happen quickly and suddenly in the novel, and Montag is frequently confused and uncertain. The form, then, with its fluidity mirrors that suddenness and that confusion and that uncertainty.

A third feature of the structure of *Fahrenheit 451* is evident in *Bradbury's use of allusions*. This technique has been studied at great length elsewhere in these Notes (see section on *Allusions*), and should not be overlooked as a unifying element in the novel.

The allusions are, in a sense, milestones marking Montag's progress in awareness. At first, feeling only vague uneasiness, Montag needs experience to bring his feelings into sharp focus. This experience is provided by the old woman who was burned with her books. The significance here is that the woman announces a kind of *credo* when she uses the words of Latimer to Cranmer. It is an enunciation which perplexes Montag; it introduces a new perspective which he must struggle to understand. Succeeding quotations—the Swift (p. 62) and the Boswell (p. 63, p. 64)—reflect Montag's confusion and lack of understanding, which is one of the most important elements of that particular section of the book. Later allusions are associated with the idea of faith, which emerges as an important element of the later stages of the novel. The faith involved is not, of course, so much orthodox religious faith as it is faith in man's capacity to prevail. It involves trust in the future. That is the significance of the words from *The Gospel according to St. Matthew* (p. 70), the reference to the *Book of Job* (p. 83), the philosophical statement from *Ecclesiastes* (p. 147) and the vision from *Revelation* (p. 147). Hence, it might be said that the allusions are, in musical terms, the theme music of the plot, that they provide the *motifs* which announces stages in plot-development.

A further element of structure is created by Bradbury's *pairing of characters*. The characters are associated with one another in a way more significant than the fact of simply being involved in the same sequence of events. They are more deeply associated with one another by a series of parallels drawn between them.

Clarisse and Mildred are obviously, in the earlier stages of the novel, intended to portray contrasting female roles. They contrast with one another in terms of qualities of character. Clarisse is full of unquenched curiosity; Mildred is apathetic and listless. Clarisse has a lively interest in people; Mildred is absorbed in the fictional world of her television 'family.' Clarisse enjoys conversation; Mildred is a victim of her Seashell radio. The wife of Montag is thus the portrait of what wives have become in the society of *Fahrenheit 451*; Clarisse is the portrait of what women might have been, if society had not wrought its destruction. It is interesting to note that when a film of the novel was made a few years ago, the same actress, Julie Christie, played the role of both Clarisse and Mildred, a fact which helped to underline the obvious parallel drawn between the two women.

Beatty and Faber are paired in a similar manner. Beatty is the practical philosopher of the new society. Shrewd, intelligent and informed, he is the voice of the *status quo*, the convinced, articulate advocate for what has happened. In opposition is Faber, standing, as it were, on the other side of Montag. Equally intelligent and informed, he opens Montag's eyes to the human aspect of experience. He becomes, in fact, almost inextricably linked with Montag, as a kind of *alter ego* struggling to be born. That relationship expresses neatly one of the novel's themes: the emergence of the new Montag. At first, Montag seems to be torn and divided into two. At one side stands Beatty, who is the representative of the 'old' Montag, Montag the fireman; at the other is Faber, who points toward the 'new' Montag, that aspect of Montag which struggles to emerge. From the opposition of the two there springs the new man (p. 92-93).

Stoneman and Black and Mrs. Bowles and Mrs. Phelps are also obviously intended to be associated with one another. All are typical of their society; all are hollow men and women. The men are silent, acquiescent pasteboard figures who do their society's work without question. The women are empty creatures, devoid of truly human feelings. Together, they create a composite picture of society.

The division of the book into three sections, the absence of chapter 'breaks', the use of allusions, the parallels drawn among the characters,—all act as structural devices which help to blend together the various aspects of the novel. Another major device in the structure is provided by *the major speeches*. Each of the major sections of the book contains a long, 'set' speech which is a key to understanding an important point of view. In the first section (pp. 49ff), the key speech is that of Captain Beatty, who patiently explains to Montag the history, development and dynamics of their society. This speech serves a number of important purposes. It enables the reader to understand the historical development which has produced the society in the novel; its emphasizes an important theme, which is the deterioration of cultural level under the impact of mass media; and it leads Montag to a greater understanding of the scope of the problem which confronts him. In the second section, Faber's speech is the key one (pp. 73ff). This speech contrasts directly with that of Beatty. It is humanistic rather than starkly sociological, and analyzes society in terms of what is needed to save it. In this way, Faber's speech gives Montag insight into what must be accomplished in order to save society from itself and into what it is that is so precious in books. Granger's speech, in section three, moves the narrative in a fresh direction, for Granger is the spokesman for the new people, those who will emerge after the holocaust (pp. 135ff). His speech, therefore, parallels that of Beatty in the first section, and extends and deepens our awareness of what Faber has been saying in the second section. All three speeches, then, set the mood for the sections in which they appear, motivate the developments in the plot and provide a context for understanding the themes of the novel. As such, they are important devices for structural unity.

There are, of course, other, minor devices which provide structure. The Hound, for instance, appears frequently in the narrative and provides a vivid element of suspense. Its appearances almost seem to take on the power of thematic images, symbolizing the menacing, threatening omnipresence of the forces against which Montag is rebelling. On occasions also, the use of irony helps to tie the structure together. For example, Granger's startling revelation, in the third section, that the exiles are book-burners casts the reader's mind back to the first section, which is full of the horror of a different kind of book-burning. However, these are minor aspects of structure, in which the main elements seem to be the division into three books, the absence of chapter headings, the use of allusions, the parallels in characterization and the three philosophical statements delivered by major characters.

Returning, then, to the statement of Virginia Woolf, with which this section of the notes began, it seems abundantly clear that Bradbury has displayed the gift which she described as "the power of combination." The various elements of the novel have been drawn together with skilful persuasiveness to present a convincing, coherent perspective.

ALLUSIONS IN FAHRENHEIT 451

Guy Montag exists in a nightmare world of the future, five hundred years hence, in which the traditional, literary basis for human life has virtually disappeared. Books are banned. Any which are now discovered are burned by the firemen, who no longer pursue their former task of extinguishing fires, but now, with hoses belching liquid fire, methodically destroy the homes and possessions of those who covet and hide books.

The origin of these social conditions emphasizes vividly the poignancy and frightfulness of the situation. For the nightmare had not been imposed upon man by a totalitarian state. It was, horrifyingly, a fate which man had brought upon himself, as Captain Beatty explained so lucidly to Montag (p. 49ff). The mass media— radio, television, the popular press—had begun the process of decline. As the mass media sought to cater to the demands and desires of a wider and wider audience, standards of taste and intellectual content began to fall. In Beatty's words, "Films and radios, magazines, books leveled down to a sort of paste pudding norm . . ." (p. 50). The masses wanted easier and faster communication; they demanded products capable of instant intellectual digestion. The public had neither time for, nor interest in anything needing careful consideration and quiet enjoyment. Consequently books, for example, were condensed until they eventually became mere short notations in reference works. When this process was accentuated by an increasing desire for personal pleasure and by an increasing emphasis upon the happiness of the present moment, the nightmare had, in fact, become a reality, without the need for repressive government measures.

This is, in the book, a frightening reality which must not be underestimated or lightly dismissed as a rather interesting background for an adventure story. The books themselves, seen merely as objects, as a series of paper pages bound in an interesting fashion, are indeed not very important. What they represent, however, is of crucial importance. For literature—fiction, philosophy, psychology, sociology, theology, and so on—provides the meaningful basis for all truly human existence. Just as the language a man uses is the mirror of that man's total humanity—his intellect, his spirit, his emotions, his ideals—so books are, in a much larger way, the mirrors of the soul of man as a species. In books, man enshrines his noblest hopes, his most secret thoughts and desires, his most considered concepts of what he perceives himself to be. In a profound sense, books *are* man. They are his confession of himself, with all his strengths and weaknesses, his ideals and his base desires, his wisdom and his ignorance, his hope and his despair, his accomplishment and his frustration, his courage and his cowardice. Thus, to each generation books offer the experience of life of those who have undertaken the human pilgrimage in days past. Thus, as books have multiplied, so has the richness of the human experience of living. Consequently, in a civilized society, a man is, in a real sense, able to live not one life but many lives. In addition, books confer upon man a further incalculable blessing; they give to him a spiritual context for his life which provides sources of thought and imagination that enable him to communicate more meaningfully with others like himself, to conceive more clearly the task of being human, and to make of his world a *home* rather than a *house*. To lose books, then, is not simply to lose objects, however valuable. To lose books is to lose an aspect of human experience which enables us to face our environment meaningfully and with confidence. To lose books means to lose a part of ourselves. That is, in some measure, the startling message of *Fahrenheit 451*, especially towards the end of the novel, when we see, strangely, that the men *are* books, and the books *are* men.

Thus it is scarcely surprising that in depicting a nightmare world without books, Bradbury should have employed quotations from literature. Further, such is the vastness of the literature available for allusions that it is no more surprising to realize that Bradbury's allusions are carefully chosen.

There are eight quotations, or groups of quotations, which demand examination. The study here considers each in turn, and from that specific consideration offers generalizations about the use of allusion in *Fahrenheit 451*.

1. Page 33:

Play the man, Master Ridley; we shall this day light such a candle, by God's grace, in England, as I trust shall never be put out.

This allusion is not literary, but historical. It refers to an incident which took place during the turbulent and violent religious controversies of sixteenth-century England. The controversy had begun with the desire of Henry VIII (1509-1547) to be divorced from his wife, Catherine of Aragon, a Spanish widow who had been married to Henry's brother, Arthur. Of course, a simple divorce was impossible. The only religiously acceptable solution was for Henry to have his marriage annulled on the grounds that he should not have been granted permission to marry his brother's widow in the first place.

When the Pope refused an annulment, Henry decided to have the annulment effected in England. Thomas Cranmer, the Archbishop of Canterbury, aided Henry, and in 1553 the king married his second wife, Anne Bolyn. The effect upon England was enormous, for the House of Commons supported Henry and in 1554 the king was declared to be the supreme Head of the Church of England. Since anti-papal feeling was strong, most of the people supported Henry, but others did not. There were rebellions in the land, and many prominent people were executed for their opposition to the king. However, the reformation of the church in England progressed gradually and inexorably over the next years. Unfortunately, the situation was complicated by problems over the succession to the throne in succeeding years. Henry's third wife gave birth to a son, Edward VI (1547-1553), who ruled only a short time after the death of his father. He was succeeded by Mary I (1553-1558), the fiercely Roman Catholic daughter of Catherine of Aragon, who attempted to restore Roman Catholicism in England. Her reign revived old controversies and was marked by violence and bloodshed as Protestants and Catholics fought for supremacy. The situation was not helped by the fact that many regarded both Mary and her half-sister, Elizabeth, as illegitimate heirs to the throne.

At this point, the name of Nicholas Ridley (c. 1500-1555) emerges. In 1553, supporting the claim to the throne of Lady Jane Grey, he preached a sermon in which he declared that both Mary and Elizabeth were illegitimate. Mary never forgave him for this action. Nor was she slow to pursue Hugh Latimer, an English bishop who had received favour from Henry VIII in spite of some accusations of heresy. Both men were doomed. On October 16, 1555, they were burned together at the stake in Oxford. As the fire was lighted, Latimer cried out, "Be of good comfort, Master Ridley, and play the man. We shall this day light such a candle, by God's grace, in England, as I trust shall never be put out."

The deaths of the martyrs, then, is a notable incident in English history. It provides a magnificent example of men who were prepared to defy the authorities who ruled them for the sake of their convictions. To them might was *not* right. Moreover, their view of their own deaths is noteworthy. Their lives were not wasted. By their example, they trusted that they would give the opposition to the queen greater resolve and encouragement.

As a result, Latimer's words become directly relevant to *Fahrenheit 451*. They are echoed by an old woman who refuses to leave her house and her books when the firemen arrive. She defies them, and even lights the kerosene herself, so that she is finally engulfed by flames. From this moment, Montag's inner torment begins. He cannot forget the woman. Thus, in the succeeding scenes of the novel, he is deeply troubled by his cold, impersonal relationship with his wife; he thinks over his encounters with Clarisse; and he is unable to report for work. The words and the old woman's action become engraved on his mind. He feels compelled to understand them. And so his rebellion begins.

The incident, with its use of Latimer's words, has accomplished important purposes for Bradbury:

- Montag's growing dissatisfaction has received focus. An objective reality has been provided for Montag in his attempt to grapple with his own feelings.

- An important step in the development of the plot has been taken. Montag's "sickness" causes Beatty's visit. It is after that that Montag turns to books to seek his answers to the problems that beset him.

- The nature of the conflict becomes more apparent. We are not confronted simply by a dissatisfied fireman. The conflict is much larger and more important. It is a conflict of values. The words of Latimer provide a setting in which we see that we are witnessing a significant battle of values, in which men may have to die, nobly but not hopelessly, for their convictions.

- The irony of the fire symbolism in the novel is underlined. The firemen use fire to destroy. But frequently in the novel the more hopeful aspect of fire symbolism is indicated. Thus, fire is associated with the Phoenix, which rises to new life from destruction by fire; Montag escapes by using fire; and at the end of the novel there is hope for new life when the old world is destroyed by fire. Similarly in the incident with the old woman— and in the original Latimer and Ridley incident—fire is not simply a means of destruction; it is the means by which a new, *spiritual* flame will be kindled.

2. Page 62:

It is computed, that eleven thousand persons have at several times suffered death rather than submit to break their eggs at the smaller end.

This quotation is taken from *Gulliver's Travels*, by Jonathan Swift. The book as a whole is a powerful satire on English life in the early eighteenth century, so that few aspects of society escape Swift's blistering attack. The political figures of the time are lampooned unmercifully; the scientists of the day are ridiculed; and the foolish pretensions of the intellectuals are flayed. Such is the bitterness of Swift's vision that Gulliver returns from his final voyage unable to stand even the smell of human beings.

The quotation appears in the first book of *Gulliver's Travels*, "A Voyage to Lilliput", in which Gulliver finds himself as a giant in a land of little people. At first, the Lilliputians seem so small and gracious that Gulliver has nothing but unqualified admiration for them. However, the hero gradually becomes aware of darker aspects of their society. He learns, for example, of a bitter feud that has divided them into two irreconcilable groups: those who eat their eggs by breaking them first at the larger end, and those who break their eggs at the smaller end. One group is unmercifully intolerant of the other, so that those who break their eggs at the larger end would rather face death than submit to the king's edict, which commands them to break their eggs at the smaller end. In itself, the episode is absurd and comical. But the satirical intent lends to it darker tones. Swift is bitingly attacking the political and religious bigotry of his own times. He is holding up to ridicule the petty and insignificant differences of opinion which he sees as dividing men into parties and sects which lack good sense, tolerance and common humanity.

It should be no surprise that Montag does not understand these words of Swift. To begin with, the entire mode of satire would be foreign to Montag. Satire demands of a reader that he be prepared to look at his society objectively. He must extricate himself from the traditional *mores* of his group and he must cast aside, even momentarily, the outlook he has learned as he has grown up in his society, so that he can see with fresh vision the customs and the ways he has hitherto accepted without question. Montag is hardly prepared for that yet. He is still confused and uncertain. At this moment all that drives him to books is his feeling of vague discontentment. Moreover, Montag is not ready yet to meet a second demand which satire makes upon the reader: satire demands that we understand and accept a completely different view of society and human life, a view usually inherent in the satirist's criticisms. To arrive at that position, the reader has not only to understand the criticisms the artist is making, but also to be prepared to accept and perhaps adopt a completely different view of human life and society. Again, Montag is hardly at a point which makes this change possible.

Thus, the use of the quotation from Swift at this point accomplishes important purposes:

- Montag's intellectual condition at this stage is underlined. So far, he is not, in a rational sense, a rebel. Emotionally, he is confused and unhappy, but as yet there is no intellectual understanding to support his feelings. He feels vaguely discontented, but books have not yet crystallized that discontent. It is therefore fitting that Montag's first excursion into books should only add to his bewilderment.

- The quotation emphasizes the enormity of Montag's task. The whole mode of political satire is utterly foreign to Montag's society. Such satire encourages discontent, whereas the world of *Fahrenheit 451* encourages contentment. Montag's society tries to banish feelings of unhappiness with drugs and diversions; satire seeks to bring such feelings to the surface and to give them expression.

- The irony apparent in the use of the quotation from Swift adds force to the contrast between the world of Montag and the world of Swift. It is ironic that Montag, seeking wisdom from books, should first choose a source which he is most unlikely to understand. The quotation transports him so swiftly (no pun intended!) from one world, which shuns controversy, to another, which lives on controversy, that he cannot hope to find instant enlightenment or immediate understanding.

3. Page 63:

We cannot tell the precise moment when friendship is formed. As in filling a vessel drop by drop, there is at last a drop which makes it run over; so in a series of kindnesses there is at last one which makes the heart run over.

This quotation is from the *Life of Dr. Johnson* (1791), written by James Boswell (1740-1795). This work is Boswell's main claim to fame, for it is his account of his friendship with one of the leading literary figures of eighteenth-century England. The writing is typical of that of the period, in that it includes some straightforward reporting, a large degree of Boswell's adulation of Dr. Johnson, many recorded aphorisms of Johnson, and Boswell's own philosophical comments. The relationship between the two men is thus one of the best-known in English literature.

Appearing at this point, the quotation serves a number of purposes:

- It signals the first positive step in Montag's efforts to understand both himself and what it is in books that makes them so valuable. Boswell's *Life of Dr. Johnson*, in this quotation, speaks about something that Montag can understand and can relate to his own experience. Thus the words immediately bring to his mind thoughts of Clarisse. Thinking over the words, he asks what is essentially a rhetorical question: "Is that what it was in the girl next door?" This moment of illumination should not be underestimated, for Guy lives in a world in which close human relationships are unknown. For example, Mildred and he cannot even remember when they first met. As Mrs. Phelps reveals later (p. 85), even within the intimacy of marriage, the partners remain "independent". Consequently, Montag's understanding of Boswell marks his growth in his understanding of the new element that Clarisse has brought into his life. What had previously seemed to him only a mysterious uneasiness about his life has now become clarified as the absence of warmth, a vacuum of absent human relationship. That is why, only a short while later (p. 68), Montag asks his wife whether the White Clown on television loves her. That is why he asks her the question which she does not even understand: "Does your 'family' love you, love you *very* much, love you with all their heart and soul, Millie?" The words from Boswell have struck a chord which will not be silenced.

- This quotation, and the one which follows, rationalizes the next stage of the development of the plot. Seeking further understanding, Montag feels compelled to talk to Faber. Realizing his numbness (p. 69), he must find help. That desire lays the groundwork for much of the future action of the novel.

- The quotation emphasizes the contrast between Montag and his wife. Boswell's words have an immediate relevance for Guy; he applies them at once to his encounter with Clarisse. On the other hand Clarisse, being a typical vacuous product of her society, is unwilling and unable to see the relevance of the words. The mention of Clarisse's name is unwelcome, summoning up an unhappy topic, and she seeks to dismiss the subject: "She's dead. Let's talk about someone alive, for goodness' sake."

- The quotation further emphasizes the contrast between Montag's world and the world as it had been. Friendship belonged to the past, to an age in which people talked meaningfully to one another. As Clarisse had explained, that world had vanished:

No front porches. My uncle says there used to be front porches. And people sat there sometimes at night, talking when they wanted to talk, rocking, and not talking when they didn't want to talk. Sometimes they just sat there and thought about things, turned things over. My uncle says the architects got rid of the front porches because they didn't look well. But my uncle says that was merely rationalizing it; the real reason, hidden underneath, might be they didn't want people sitting like that, doing nothing, rocking, talking; that was the wrong *kind* of social life. People talked too much. And they had time to think. So they ran off with the porches." (pp. 57-58)

Now, the aim of society was to "get people up and running around."

4. Page 64:

That favourite subject, Myself.

These words are again from Boswell and appear in a letter he wrote to Temple on July 26, 1763.

The quotation at this point is worthy of note because:

- It is the only occasion on which Mildred claims to understand something which Guy does not. She declares unequivocally that she understands *that* one (p. 64), whereas Montag is puzzled, and for very good reason:

"But Clarisse's favourite subject wasn't herself. It was everyone else and me.

Of course, the difference in the reactions to the quotation marks marks the difference in their points of view. It cannot really be said that Mildred understands. She understands in a very limited way, a way which distorts Boswell's words. For she applies them to the emphasis in her own society upon selfish pleasure. Her world teaches self-indulgent immersion in the happiness of the present moment and the importance of the individual's freedom from anxiety. Thus she sees Boswell's words as expressing that kind of selfishness. What neither she nor Montag understands is that the words are based on a concept of the rich inner life of the individual. The real person has a wealth of emotions, thoughts, opinions, experiences and relationships which feeds his inner life and contributes to his individuality. Without that, he is not truly a real "I" able to enter into significant relationship with other real individuals. Thus, for example, Clarisse is able to take an interest in others only because she is, within herself, a credible person.

- The obvious irony in the different reactions of Mildred and Montag to the quotation adds depth and pungency to our understanding of both characters. We are able to see more sharply the contrast between their points of view and to understand more clearly the position of each.

- Mildred's reaction to the quotation emphasizes again the nature of the world in *Fahrenheit 451*. Further elaboration of that point is not necessary, since it has already been made clear in ex plaining the different ways in which Mildred and Guy react to Boswell's words.

5. Page 70:

Consider the lilies of the field.

This is a quotation from the Bible, and in particular from Jesus' famous Sermon on the Mount in the *Gospel according to St. Matthew*. It is worthwhile at this point to recall the section from which the quotation is taken:

> Therefore I say unto you, Take no thought for your life, what ye shall eat, or what ye shall drink; nor yet for your body, what ye shall put on. Is not the life more than meat, and the body than raiment?
>
> Behold the fowls of the air: for they sow not, neither do they reap, nor gather into barns; yet your heavenly Father feedeth them. Are ye not much better than they?
>
> Which of you by taking thought can add one cubit unto his stature?
>
> And why take ye thought for raiment? Consider the lilies of the field, how they grow; they toil not, neither do they spin:
>
> And yet I say unto you, That even Solomon in all his glory was not arrayed like one of these.
>
> Wherefore, if God so clothe the grass of the field, which today is, and tomorrow is cast into the oven, shall he not much more clothe you, O ye of little faith?
>
> Therefore, take no thought, saying, What shall we eat? or, What shall we drink? or, Wherewithal shall we be clothed?
>
> (For after all these things do the Gentiles seek:) for your heavenly Father knoweth that ye have need of all these things.
>
> But seek ye first the kingdom of God, and his righteousness; and all these things shall be added unto you.   (Chapter 6, vv. 25-33)

The Sermon obviously has a double massage. On the one hand, it exhorts men to deliver themselves from the frenzy of everyday concerns, from the anxiety about physical needs which blinds them to any other aspect of reality. On the other hand, its positive message is that men should be aware of the spiritual reality which is hidden by the facade of material concerns. In a sense, it is saying that present must give way to the eternal; the transient must surrender to the permanent.

Montag reads these words from the Bible when he is on the subway, making his way frantically to see Faber. He is distraught. He has been unable to communicate meaningfully with Mildred. What he has read in books has so far only succeeded in confusing him, so that his endeavour seems as futile as trying to fill a sieve with sand. Harried and anxious, he finds the atmosphere on the train no help to him, for his ears are assailed by the radio, which is shrieking a nonsensical jingle urging people to buy Denham's Dentifrice. At this point, the use of the words from the Sermon on the Mount accomplishes a number of purposes:

- The tension within Montag is emphasized. The Biblical words and the words of the inane commercial appear in a kind of counterpoint, each with its own urgent and distinctive rhythm. The "music" goes back and forth, tormenting Montag until he bolts from the subway in a frantic effort to find respite. Thus the two "tunes" represent the two sides of the conflict within Montag: the voice of the mindless present world and the voice of a world which he is as yet only beginning to comprehend.

- The nature of Montag's society is underlined by the contrast which the Biblical words present. In this world, the present is all that matters; the present moment is all-important. In contrast, the words of the Sermon on the Mount indicate a different view of human life and activity. They portray a new vision, a view of life in which things are seen from the viewpoint of eternity and in which feverish anxiety is replaced by trusting calm.

6. Page 83:

The Book of Job.

This allusion is different from the others which have so far been examined. The reference faces us, not with a single quotation, but simply with the mention of an entire work, the Book of Job in the Old Testament.

The title is mentioned by Faber, as Montag is returning home after visiting the professor. Montag cannot yet see the way ahead. He no longer feels himself to be a member of his own society, but he has not yet arrived at an understanding of what his new role demands of him. Faber, by means of the tiny radio transmitter, tries to reassure him. He tells the fireman that he must not be impatient, even though he has not yet started acting independently. Montag must learn to "travel blind for awhile" and trust in Faber. He must have faith. Finally, Faber offers to read to Montag; the reading he chooses is the Book of Job.

The choice is significant. The Book of Job, which appears in the Old Testament, is a poetical work which is a hymn of praise to faith. Job, a "perfect and an upright man", is tried and tested by God at the urging of Satan, who declares that when adversity strikes Job will curse God. Thus Job loses his property, his family and even his health. In this time of trial not even his friends are a source of solace, and Job bemoans his fate. However, he endures, and at last acknowledges humbly the sovereignty of God:

> I know that thou canst do everything, and that no thought can be witholden from thee.
> Who is he that hideth counsel without knowledge? therefore have I uttered that I understood not; things too wonderful for me, which I knew not.
> Hear, I beseech thee, and I will speak: I will demand of thee, and declare thou unto me.
> I have heard of thee by the hearing of the ear: but now my eye seeth thee.
> Wherefore I abhor myself, and repent in dust and ashes.
> (Chapter 42, verses 2-6)

Thus, in the great struggle between evil and good in human life, Job learns that the role of man is to trust.

The use of the Book of Job at this particular point in *Fahrenheit 451* is obviously appropriate for a number of reasons:

- It indicates a turmoil in the mind of Montag which must be resolved as the plot develops. That the turmoil is incapable of easy resolution soon becomes apparent in the following scene, in which Montag reads to his wife's friends. However, by contrast, Faber's urging of caution and his attempt to calm Montag with the use of the Book of Job, effectively highlights the tension and the reader's awareness of the approaching crisis.

- The use of the Book of Job effectively introduces the element of Biblical imagery, which plays such an important role near the end of the novel. This imagery injects into the book a new dimension. While it might be an exaggeration to label that dimension as 'eternal', nevertheless the religious element does force the reader to see the conflict in the book against a larger background. The conflict then becomes, not simply one man's struggle against his society, but the struggle of the whole race to be truly human. Bradbury does, of course, see the struggle in that wider sense, for at the end we are left with the confidence that the "healing of nations" will take place. Hence, the use of the Book of Job—and of all of the biblical imagery—accomplishes two purposes in one: it adds a new and important perspective to the conflict, and it sounds a note of optimism for the future.

7. Page 90:

The Sea of Faith
Was once, too, at the full, and round earth's shore
Lay like the folds of a bright girdle furled.
But now I only hear
Its melancholy, long, withdrawing roar,
Retreating, to the breath
Of the night-wind, down the vast edges drear
And naked shingles of the world.

Ah, love, let us be true
To one another! for the world, which seems
To lie before us like a land of dreams,
So various, so beautiful, so new,
Hath really neither joy, nor love, nor light,
Nor certitude, nor peace, nor help for pain;
And we are here as on a darkling plain
Swept with confused alarms of struggle and flight,
Where ignorant armies clash by night.

These are two stanzas from "Dover Beach", a poem by Matthew Arnold (1822-1888). It is a work which expresses succinctly the typical romantic pessimism of Arnold, for here, standing on the shore, faced by the apparent night-beauty of the ocean, he sees, not a vision of attractiveness and hope, but a vision of sadness and despair. The sea is not the symbol of the "bright girdle" of faith surrounding the life of man; the ocean is in retreat, its sound a "melancholy, long, withdrawing roar", from the "naked shingles of the world", where human beings struggle in confusion "as on a darkling plain." In the midst of this despairing vision, the poet addresses his companion, declaring that their love must save them.

This use of "Dover Beach" is interesting for a number of reasons:

- It delineates clearly Montag's position. It is not by accident that he reads this poem at this particular moment. True, he does not choose it to read to Mildred's friends; Mildred makes the choice. But she makes this particular choice because Montag had been reading the poem earlier that day. Thus, in some way the poem has been meaningful to Montag. In actual fact, it is entirely appropriate that it should have appealed to him. For the poem expresses two important insights. On the one hand, it expresses an insight which goes beyond the deceptive attractiveness of the world, seeing that the world, which *seems* to be like "a land of dreams", is actually a place where there is "neither joy, nor love, nor light." On the other hand, the poem is an impressive expression of the importance of human relationship in general and of the importance of human love in particular. Thus the poem is an acutely relevant expression of Montag's own experience. He, too, has perceived the deceptive attractiveness of the world for what it is . . . sheer deceptiveness. He, too, in pondering his relationship with Mildred, has come to appreciate the new dimension which truly human relationship can give to life. One might declare with a good deal of accuracy, then, that Arnold's romantic pessimism has struck an answering chord in the romantic pessimism of Montag. Through this, the reader is able to understand more clearly the spiritual condition of the hero.

- In the second place, the use of the poem indicates vividly the emptiness of Mildred. Montag had read the poem aloud earlier that day, but it had meant nothing to Mildred. She chose it for Montag to read to her friends because she was sure that they would not understand it. She was confident that it was a prime example of the folly to be found in books. All that she could remember of it was that "it goes umpty-tumpty-ump" (p. 89). After the reading, she made a desperate attempt to make her friends happy again, suggesting that they turn on television and have a party. Mildred is obviously a typical product of her society, one who will never understand the spiritual crisis which her husband suffers. She is incapable of change.

- The poem underlines the nature of the world depicted in *Fahrenheit 451*. Arnold's picture of the world obviously relates to the world of the novel, where dark reality looms just beneath the superficial glitter of the happiness cult. The pills, the 'family', the invited brushes with death, the suicides,—all help to banish the voice of reality for the citizens of the novel. But the reality is there, as Montag comes to realize.

- The use of the poem in this scene illustrates powerfully the potential effect of literature. The women are not willing listeners. Yet they do not remain unaffected by the reading of the poem. Mrs. Phelps is reduced to tears. Mrs. Bowles is angry, because poetry and tears always accompany one another. They may not have understood all that they had heard, yet the poem must have communicated in some way, in order to provoke their violent reactions. Perhaps this is a vivid illustration of T. S. Eliot's statement of poetry's appeal to the "auditory imagination." Thus, the explanation might go that poetry can speak to us, even when we do not understand it, by the power of its sounds, which resurrect in us thoughts and feelings that had seemed long-dead or even non-existent. The long-buried human feelings ot Mrs. Phelps and Mrs. Bowles had not escaped the voice which spoke to them. Though the feelings were unwelcome, they had undoubtedly responded. In that lies one source of hope in the novel.

8. Page 96-97:

The nature of the allusions in these pages is different from that of the allusions whichhave preceded or which follow. The other allusions present single quotations or references; in these pages, a number of quotations are given in pairs.

The reason for the difference is easily apparent on consideration of the context. Montag had returned to the fire station after hiding his books in the garden at home. He was now resolved. He was committed to books in a way that he had not been previously. Thus he looked forward confidently to the future, relying on the assistance he would have from Faber: "Even now he could feel the start of the long journey, the leave-taking, the going-away from the self he had been." (p. 93) However, at the station he had to encounter Captain Beatty, who with cunning insight realized what was happening to Montag. Consequently, the Captain set out to confuse and upset Montag. The tone of the encounter is set by the Captain's greeting: "Well, here comes a very strange beast which in all tongues is called a fool" (p. 94). Beatty then related a dream he was supposed to have had, in which Montag and he engaged in "a furious debate about books", during which they exchanged contradictory quotations from books. Beatty then proceeded to confuse Montag by expressing the literary contradictions, summing up his attack with the cynical observation: ". . . I was doing a terrible thing in using the very books you clung to, to rebut you on every hand, on every point! What traitors books can be! you think they're backing you up, and they turn on you." As a result, Montag was hammered into trance-like submission, so that he "sat like a carved white stone."

The scene is impressive, and Bradbury's use of the large number of quotations which refute one another serves a variety of purposes:

- Obviously, the nature of Montag's main adversary has been emphasized. Captain Beatty is by no means an unworthy opponent. He is both shrewd and knowledgeable. He knows very well the crisis through which Montag is passing. Furthermore, in spite of his job he is well acquainted with the books he has burned. He is far more literate than Montag; he has the literary ammunition necessary to reduce the fireman to a state of bewilderment. This glimpse of Beatty thus obviously confirms the impression we received of him earlier, when he had explained to Montag the origin of the present state of society (pp. 49-57). Beatty is thus a dangerous opponent because of his cleverness and learning.

- The two-fold aspect of the use of the quotations here contributes effectively to the tension of the scene. The quotations lash back and forth, now enunciating a positive statement, now denying the statement. This statement refutation movement in the scene mirrors very well the confusion of Montag. He has committed himself irrevocably to books, but he has yet much to learn. He is not yet the new Montag, the 'real' Montag able to cope without the assistance of Faber. Thus the very technique Beatty uses is the technique that Montag cannot be expected to handle. Therefore, the two-fisted movement of the quotations both increases the tempo of the scene and also adds ironic force to the confrontation.

9. Page 147:

To everything there is a season . . . A time to break down, and a time to build up . . . A time to keep silence and a time to speak.

These words are from *Ecclesiastes*, a book of the Old Testament, and appear in Chapter 3 of that work. The use of this book is of particular interest. For *Ecclesiastes* is not so much a book expressing hope for the future as it is a work which expresses the author's profound cynicism. He has experienced life to the full, and his conclusion is that "all is vanity" (Chapter 1, verse 2). Human wisdom, pleasure, wealth and work,—all are examined and found to be futile, because man lives in the midst of a world which can only teach pessimism and despair when one views the sufferings of the oppressed, the loneliness of humankind and the cruelty of the despots. Faced with such a dark vision, the conclusion of the writer is inevitable:

> There is nothing better for a man, than that he should eat and drink, and that he should make his soul enjoy good in his labour.
>
> (Chapter 2, verse 24)

Or again:

> Then I commended mirth, because a man hath no better thing under the sun, than to eat, and to drink, and to be merry.
>
> (Chapter 8, verse 15)

Thus at first sight it may seem strange that Bradbury should have chosen to make allusion to this particular book so close to the end of *Fahrenheit 451*. Montag and his new companions had obviously sacrificed much and suffered much for their convictions. They had endured for the sake of the future. How, then, could the use of the pessimistic Ecclesiastes be appropriate at this stage of the novel?

The answer to that question is found by considering another aspect of *Ecclesiastes*. In one aspect, the pessimism of the author finds its source in his view of history. He had rejected orthodox belief in the hereafter and in his work shows belief in a cyclical view of history. In this view, history and nature are seen to involve a circular movement which repeats itself perpetually. The simplest analogy for this point of view is to be found in nature, for the seasons of the year, involving the "death" that winter brings and the "rebirth" of spring, revolve in a constantly repeated cycle. So in the society of men there is a constant rise and fall in the achievements of man. This view can give rise to optimism or pessimism, depending on one's emphasis. In "good" times, it can be a source of pessimism, for decline in the future is seen to be inevitable as the wheel of fortune turns slowly but inexorably. In bad times, this view can be seen to have hopeful aspects, for the future will bring better things with the same kind of inevitability. Obviously, at the end of *Fahrenheit 451* it is this latter emphasis which finds expression. The conclusion of the book is intended to be encouraging rather than discouraging.

The reference to the book of Ecclesiastes thus stresses an important aspect of Bradbury's novel. His work does seem to suggest a cyclical view of human history. This view is expressed most clearly by Granger:

> ... And when the war's over, some day, some year, the books can be written again, the people will be called in, one by one, to recite what they know and we'll set it up in type until another Dark Age, when we might have to do the whole damn thing over again.   (p. 137)

However, that insight is not intended to be a source of pessimism. It is seen, by Granger and evidently by Bradbury himself, as wonderful evidence of the capacity of man to endure. Again, Granger expresses this aspect most clearly:

> ... But that's the wonderful thing about man; he never gets so discouraged or disgusted that he gives up doing it all over again, because he knows very well it is important and *worth* the doing.   (p. 137)

The use of this allusion to *Ecclesiastes* is, then, of crucial importance to the novel:

- In common with the other biblical imagery, it helps to set the conflict in the novel against a larger background. It provides a new, wider perspective from which we can judge the significance of the events.

- It injects a message of hope into a grim situation. The gloom is viewed as being merely temporary; it will pass. Man, in the end, will prevail against the forces that would rob him of his humanity; the future is bright with promise. That is not to say that the future is unstained by threats of impending disaster. But, in the most profound sense, Bradbury would seem to have us believe that where there is life there is hope. Man himself is the hope.

- The allusion focuses the emphasis where it ought to be . . . upon man himself. Cycles of life and decay may be inevitable, times of achievement give way inexorably to times of decline, but throughout all man endures. As Granger observes, the wonderful thing about man is that he "never gets so discouraged or disgusted that he gives up doing it all over again." That message is, of course, both a source of warning and of wisdom. Truly taken to heart, it means that we must cherish the aspects of our humanity which endure. The transient things of the moment must not totally occupy our energies. We must make our contribution by safeguarding the sensitivities which make us human, so that when the darkness descends there might still be sources of hope which will win through to the new day.

10. Page 147:

And on either side of the river was there a tree of life, which bare twelve manner of fruits, and yielded her fruit every month; and the leaves of the tree were for the healing of the nations.

Again, the source of this quotation is biblical. The words can be found in their context in *The Revelation of St. John the Divine*, the last book of the New Testament:

And he shewed me a pure river of water of life, clear as crystal, proceeding out of the throne of God and of the Lamb.
In the midst of the street of it, and on either side of the river, was there the tree of life, which bare twelve manner of fruits, and yielded her fruit every month: and the leaves of the tree were for the healing of the nations.
And there shall be no more curse: but the throne of God and of the Lamb shall be in it; and his servants shall serve him:
And they shall see his face; and his name shall be in the foreheads.
And there shall be no night there; and they need no candle, neither light of the sun; for the Lord God giveth them light: and they shall reign for ever and ever.   (Chapter 22, verses 1-5)

The nature of the book of Revelation can be clearly seen from this extended quotation. It obviously belongs in the stream of apocalyptic literature. That is, it deals with those events and situations which will be known when God at last rules supreme on earth as in heaven. For apocalyptic literature raises the vision of men from the discouraging, harrowing experiences of earthly life to the wonders and promises of what God will bring to pass. The *Revelation* is firmly in that tradition of writing. Written at a time (c. A.D. 96) when the author felt sure that the Church was about to experience an age of renewed persecution, it sought to encourage men with the bright promise that the future held to those who trusted in God.

The use of *Revelation* so near the end of the novel is important:

- Again, the biblical context contributes a larger perspective to the novel, as has been observed previously.

- The words from *Revelation* enable Bradbury to end with a note of hopefulness. The future is bright with promise, even though disaster has struck the cities of men. And that hope is not only the hope of the immediate future. In the long range, man has solace, for the vision presents a tree of life which bears fruit perpetually. The tree yields its fruit *every month*—not only in seasons of fruitfulness, but also in seasons of unfruitfulness. Thus, the darkness may descend upon man once more, but even in the midst of the gloom there shines the light of promise.

SUMMARY

It can hardly be denied that the allusions in *Fahrenheit 451* make important contributions to the novel. In general, those contributions may be summarised as follows:

a. The allusions are employed in a way which clarifies the stages in the development of the plot. Beginning with Latimer's words and ending with the quotation from *Revelation*, we are able in the intermediate stages to see the progression of Montag's searching slowly take form. From confusion and lack of understanding, he proceeds to awareness, each stage of his illumination being illustrated by an illusion which helps to depict his frame of mind at a particular time. The allusions are thus an important feature of the plot-structure.

b. The allusions clarify the central conflict of the novel. By contrast, for example, they help us to see the horrifying depersonalization of life which is the leading feature of society in *Fahrenheit 451*. The books speak with a human voice; society speaks with a mechanical voice-box. Further, as this section of these notes has emphasized on a number of occasions, the allusions help to emphasize the nature of the conflict in the novel. By infusing a wider perspective into the novel, the allusions, and particularly the biblical allusions, create a larger hero for the novel; the tragic hero becomes, not just Montag, but the whole human race. The conflict is seen, then, as being, not one man's struggle against a particular society, but in a sense the struggle of the race to achieve a vision of the future. The cyclical view stresses that this is not a struggle to be fought once and won once. It is a kind of constant warfare in which man must be ever-vigilant to defeat the forces that would deprive him of his humanity.

c. The allusions are frequently used as a device to portray the frightening emptiness of society in *Fahrenheit 451*. The qualities which the quotations express are absent from that society. Friendship, sacrifice, a sense of the self, the power of human love, intuition of the future,—all are aspects of human existence which the allusions present, but which none of the characters, except those whom Montag joins, can even comprehend. The attitude of the citizens finds its voice in Mildred who, uncomprehending, declares: "Books aren't people. You read and I look all around, but there isn't *anybody*!" (p. 64)

THEME AND PURPOSE

In undertaking a discussion of the purpose of *Fahrenheit 451*, it is salutary to read, first, what Ray Bradbury has written about the *genre* he has chosen. Bradbury, as we can see from his biography (cp the section of these Notes on *The Author*), has had a life-long interest in the world of fantasy, and his comments on that interest are enlightening and informative. He writes:

I think that science-fiction and fantasy offer the liveliest, freshest approaches to many of our problems today, and I always hope to write in this vivid and vigorous form, saying what I think about philosophy and sociology in our immediate future. An ancestor of mine, Mary Bradbury, was tried as a witch in Salem in the seventeenth-century; from her, I suppose, I get my concern and dedicated interest in freedom from fear and a detestation for thought-investigation or thought-control of any sort. Science-fiction is a wonderful hammer; I intend to use it when and if necessary, to bark a few shins or knock a few heads, in order to make people leave people alone.

In this statement, which appears to be Bradbury's *credo* as a writer, we must be aware of the strong vein of social concern which is emphasized and re-emphasized. Bradbury obviously does not regard the form of writing he has chosen to be merely diverting and entertainment. What he has chosen to do is motivated by a powerful concern for his society and its life. He is not, in the light of this statement, interested in writing science-fiction because it gives free rein to the imagination in the invention of miracles as yet unknown to man. The *genre* is of interest to him partly on account of its vividness and freshness, but also partly on account of the opportunity it affords to say what he has to say upon topics that are far from frivolous and diverting—philosophy and sociology. Fantasy may be the *genre*, but the purpose is social comment. And he intends powerful social comment, of the kind that may bruise shins and knock heads. The total effect is to be that of a hammer.

That *Fahrenheit 451* fulfils the author's purpose by being socially relevant is beyond question. The novel offers a biting commentary, not upon the future, but upon the present. This is the whole import of Beatty's important speech in the book. The Captain is explaining how his society evolved to its present state, but in the process he shows us the seeds of that future clearly in our present. Their society, he explains, really began in the twentieth-century. Motion pictures, radio and television were the origin of the process, for they provided means whereby mass communication could be undertaken. That mass communication proved to be admirably useful when the burgeoning population made demands for entertainment and amusement. The mass media complied by providing mass culture. The effect of satisfying that demand was enormous. The level of culture declined, since the common denominator of interest was low, in view of the size of the audience. Moreover, in order to avoid offending large sections of their audience, the mass media avoided dissension and controversy. Magazines became "a nice blend of vanilla tapioca", and books became "dishwater". When there was added to this situation the growing pace of life in the twentieth-century, the speed of the process of degeneration quickened. The public had no time for books; cartoons and comics were of more interest because of their instant communication. At that point, it is obvious from what Beatty says, the future was already well-established. The people had surrendered their culture. They were already a little less than human. None of this, it is worth noting, is intended to be a description of Beatty's world. He is describing the twentieth-century—*our* century!

It is instructive to ask at this point whether Bradbury's interpretation of our time is accurate and just. It is a serious question indeed to ponder whether we are becoming a mindless generation, whether the level of culture is declining in our time before the onslaught of the media, whether our cultural resources can withstand the onslaughts on taste.

In seeking an answer to these problems, it must be emphasized that Bradbury's depiction of our present situation is by no means an eccentric or unusual one. For example, Hyman H. Goldin, writing in *Public Television*, which is the Carnegie Commission. His report on educational television, published in 1967, writes about commercial television in this way:

> . . . As for the system's performance in the field of mass entertainment, it is under constant criticism. Most of the complaints can be summed up in charges that television entertainment is pitched to a standard of taste which is too low, that is produced by formula and frequently is trite and uninvolving, that it fails by its own proclaimed standard of being somewhat ahead of popular taste and in fact *tends to deteriorate the standards of public taste.*　　(p. 230 Italics added.)

Goldin describes precisely the situation Beatty explained as producing the world of *Fahrenheit 451*. Moreover, it is a commonly emphasized phenomenon of our times. The words of David Karp, in his essay *TV Shows Are Not Supposed To Be Good*, might well have been spoken by Beatty:

> Why is TV so bad and still so successful? Because American taste— and the taste of the English, French, Germans and other idiots—is awful. Lincoln is reputed to have remarked that God must have loved the common people, since He made so many of them. Lincoln must have made the remark when he was speaking as a politician. Politicians adore the common man and so does Proctor & Gamble. *The commoner, the better.* The saddening truth about television is that the audience is out there, listening, watching, in numbers which shake us and they haven't reached out to turn off their sets. They switch channels and the networks are as sensitive to the clicking of those switches as they are to the very air they breathe. But the sets stay on. More and more of them.　　(Italics added)

Similarly, another commentator, Joseph Wood Krutch, in his essay *Can We Survive the Fun Explosion*?, sees a trend away from the hard demands of culture toward the emphasis on pleasure. His emphasis is not so much on the decline in standards which follows mass pleasure-seeking, as on the horrifying effects of the resulting boredom:

> Is it—or isn't it—a cause for surprise that the age of fun should be also both an age of violence and (among a conspicuous group of intellectuals) an age of philosophical despair? Fun, violence and despair seem at first sight to make an unexpected trio but perhaps there is a natural relation. Since you can't possibly have fun all the time, since seeking it too persistently and too exclusively is a sure way of finding boredom and frustration instead, perhaps pessimism is the inevitable reaction of the thoughtful, and violence the inevitable reaction

of those who do not analyze their frustrations . . . When, a few months ago, a Tucson youth drove an icepick into the back of a school maintenance worker and then said he had no idea why he assaulted a man against whom he had no grudge, the shocking thing was that, in a sense, the incident was too typical of what one reads about almost daily to cause shock. And one wonders again if the reaction against the boredom of a fun-oriented society does not have something to do with the situation.

The "unexpected trio" of fun, violence and despair loom large in the pages of *Fahrenheit 451*. There, happiness at any cost has produced a violent society, in which children kill one another and in which senseless slaughter is wrought upon the roads. Moreover, despair is everywhere, a fact we soon comprehend on learning of the numerous suicides among the citizens.

Bradbury's novel is obviously not pure fantasy. He is writing, as these commentators make clear, about *our* world. With the vision of a prophet, he is warning of our "paste pudding norm" that passes for culture and of our haste to elevate the importance of the pleasure principle against the hard facts of human existence. In this, he is accomplishing an important purpose of his writing. His writing has succeeded in becoming a "hammer" which he can use against those people and forces which are producing what he sees to be a dangerous situation. *Fahrenheit 451* is Bradbury's vehicle for protest. The novel is not really a work of science fiction, if that means simply an imaginative fantasy about the future. It is a novel of social comment, imaginative perhaps, but also relevant, insistent and passionate.

Yet it must not be assumed that that purpose is wholly negative. The novel does not simply destroy our pretensions and expose to criticism our drift to intellectual oblivion. A second purpose infuses the pages of the novel with confident hopefulness. That second purpose seems to be Bradbury's desire to express his faith in man. The situation may be critical in his view, and the future may be ominous. But Bradbury expresses positively his faith in man to survive the disasters which he brings upon himself. The book ends on a note of hope, with Montag's quoting from *Revelation*. Further, in the words of Granger we constantly hear the affirmative message. It is simple yet undeniably insistent:

. . . that's the wonderful thing about man; he never gets so discouraged or disgusted that he gives up doing it all over again, because he knows very well it is important and *worth* the doing.   (p. 137)

Thus, *Fahrenheit 451* presents us with a cyclical view of human history. Its pages say that Dark Ages come and go. But it is in the shining intervals that man shows his glory. He persists; he rebuilds; and he continues to hope. As Granger says, "We know all the damn silly things we've done for a thousand years and as long as we know that and always have it around where we can see it, some day we'll stop making the goddam funeral pyres and jumping in the middle of them."

This is the same kind of noble affirmation of faith that William Faulkner proclaimed on receiving the Nobel Prize for Literature:

> . . . I decline to accept the end of man. It is easy enough to say that man is immortal simply because he will endure; that when the last ding-dong of doom has clanged and faded from the last worthless rock hanging tideless in the last red and dying evening, that even then there will still be one more sound: that of his puny inexhaustible voice still talking. I refuse to accept this. I believe that man will not merely endure: he will prevail. He is immortal, not because he alone among creatures has an inexhaustible voice, but because he has a soul, a spirit capable of compassion and sacrifice and endurance. The poet's, the writer's, duty is to write about these things. It is his privilege to help man endure by lifting his heart, by reminding him of the courage and honour and hope and pride and compassion and pity and sacrifice which have been the glory of his past. The poet's voice need not merely be the record of man, it can be one of the props, the pillars to help him endure and prevail.

That, in poetical prose, is the kind of faith that *Fahrenheit 451* would leave with us.

The purposes, then, are clear:

1. On the one hand, Bradbury is warning us against the casual drift from culture that he sees in our society. In common with other contemporary observers, he does not view that drift as harmless or insignificant. Culture is the measure of man's humanity. Without it, he is not truly human.

2. Bradbury affirms his faith in man. As we see in the novel, destruction may be visited upon him, but he persists. From the ashes, he rises hopefully to new life. Thus, the illumination is never lost. In this, man not only endures; he prevails.

From these purposes, the themes of the novel emerge:

1. The emptiness of modern mass culture, which lowers standards of discrimination to sub-human levels;

2. The horrifying effects of a cultural vacuum, in terms of violence and despair;

3. The saving instinct of the human being toward things that transcend the merely material;

4. The cyclical view of human history. This view can be conceived as a source of pessimism. But in the novel it is seen as a source of consolation. Though darkness may descend, the light is sure to follow. In the midst of society there is always, by some peculiar grace, that company, however small, which remembers and cherishes the things that make us human.

REVIEW QUESTIONS

1. Examine carefully the speech of Captain Beatty and explain, in your own words the process which has produced the society of *Fahrenheit 451*.

2. Describe those features of society in the novel which impress you as being (a) inventive and imaginative and (b) horrifying.

3. Write a short essay in which you show the relationship between the setting and the themes.

4. Choosing a "pair" of characters, explainhow Bradbury draws a parallel between them. Your answer should include a detailed portrait of each character and offer an explanation of the reason for relating them to one another.

5. Explain in detail the function of *two* allusions in the novel.

6. Bradbury claims a social purpose for his writing. Justify this claim by an analysis of one aspect of *Fahrenheit 451*.

7. What does Montag learn from Faber? How well does he learn? Refer to specific conversations and events in the novel.

8. Justify the statement that Faber represents the *alter ego* of Montag.

9. *Fahrenheit 451* has been described as prophetic. In what sense do you regard this as a just description?

10. Describe three examples of the use of irony in the novel. In each case, explain the contribution that the use of irony makes to the narrative.